Reclaiming Caring
in Teaching and
Teacher Education

Rethinking Childhood

Joe L. Kincheloe and Janice A. Jipson
General Editors

Vol. 24

PETER LANG
New York • Washington, D.C./Baltimore • Bern
Frankfurt am Main • Berlin • Brussels • Vienna • Oxford

Lisa S. Goldstein

Reclaiming Caring
in Teaching and
Teacher Education

PETER LANG
New York • Washington, D.C./Baltimore • Bern
Frankfurt am Main • Berlin • Brussels • Vienna • Oxford

Library of Congress Cataloging-in-Publication Data

Goldstein, Lisa S.
Reclaiming caring in teaching and teacher education / Lisa S. Goldstein.
p. cm. – (Rethinking childhood; vol. 24)
Includes bibliographical references and index.
1. Moral education. 2. Teaching–Philosophy. 3. Education–Moral
and ethical aspects. 4. Teachers–Training of. I. Title. II. Series.
LC268 .G584 372.1102'01–dc21 2001038892
ISBN 0-8204-5518-0
ISSN 1086-7155

Die Deutsche Bibliothek-CIP-Einheitsaufnahme

Goldstein, Lisa S.:
Reclaiming caring in teaching and teacher education / Lisa S. Goldstein.
–New York; Washington, D.C./Baltimore; Bern;
Frankfurt am Main; Berlin; Brussels; Vienna; Oxford: Lang.
(Rethinking childhood; Vol. 24)
ISBN 0-8204-5518-0

Cover design by Lisa Dillon

The paper in this book meets the guidelines for permanence and durability
of the Committee on Production Guidelines for Book Longevity
of the Council of Library Resources.

Printed in the United States of America

With love to

Noah and Sam

Lennon

&

Tim

Table of Contents

Acknowledgments

In my jewelry box I have a special necklace. Made of a Shrinky-Dink strung on pink yarn, the necklace has been sitting among my pearls, my broken wristwatches, my too-fancy-to-wear earrings for more than a decade. One side is covered with colored squiggles and says "I love you, Mrs. G." The other side says "Sara Goldband."

When Sara gave me that necklace, she was 7 years old and I was her second grade teacher. I treasure this necklace because it evokes powerful memories of the joy and connection I experienced in my years as a classroom teacher. More importantly, the necklace reminds me of something Sara said when she learned that I was leaving teaching to go to graduate school to study teacher education.

Since I was the best teacher in the world, Sara explained logically, it made sense for me to get a job teaching people how to be great teachers. Although I was certainly not the best teacher in the world, I made a promise to Sara and her classmates that I would do my very best to help people become loving, creative, intelligent teachers. This book reflects that commitment.

I want to express my gratitude to the preservice teachers in this study and to all the other preservice teachers with whom I have worked and from whom I have learned. Thanks also to my graduate students for their role in my theorizing about teacher education. And, as ever, I must thank "Martha George" and Nel Noddings for helping to build the foundation on which my work rests.

Several of my colleagues deserve special recognition for their direct contributions to this book: Jim Scheurich for suggesting that I write a book about caring in teacher education; Vickie Lake and Debra Freedman for data analysis and work on the presentations and journal articles that preceded some of the chapters; Dwight Rogers for coining the phrase "gentle smiles and warm hugs" and allowing me to use it so freely; Dianne Pape for her careful reading of the manuscript; Stuart Reifel for his patience, humor, and encouragement; and Laura Havlick for her efforts to keep things running smoothly. Thanks are also due to Chris Myers, Jackie Pavlovic, and the folks at Peter Lang.

Portions of chapter 1 are reprinted by permission of the author and the Association for Childhood Education International. Some of the material included in chapter 2 are copyright (1999) by the American Educational Research Association and were adapted with permission from the publisher. Portions of chapter 3 and chapter 4 appeared in an earlier form in *Teaching & Teacher Education* and appears here with the permission of the author and Elsevier Science.

I could not have written this book without the generosity, flexibility, and understanding of my family. Thanks to Rich and Kellie, to my kids Noah and Sam, and to Lennon my beloved bull-dog. Extra special thanks to Tim Birchard—for little things like bringing me Diet Coke and Dubble Bubble at crucial moments, for big things like moving a sofa upstairs into my office so the dog would stay next to me as I wrote, and for enormous efforts like formatting the entire book. I could not have asked for a more supportive and encouraging partner.

Introduction

Caring has become a buzzword in education. The National Association for the Education of Young Children's newest standards for developmentally appropriate practice (Bredekamp & Copple, 1997) make explicit the important role played by caring in early childhood learning environments. Journals have devoted entire issues to the theme of caring (see Lipsitz, 1996). Aspiring to move beyond the occasional themed issue, a scholarly journal was created to focus entirely on issues relating to caring in school contexts (see Curcio & First, 1995); a number of books have been published along similar lines (Charney, 1991; Prillaman, Eaker & Kendrick, 1994). In the past decade, journal articles have described the importance of caring in the teaching of mathematics (Robicheaux, 1996), science (Sickle & Spector, 1996), social studies (Alter, 1995; Rust, 1994), language arts (Lamme & McKinley, 1992; Rasinski, 1990), and educational technology (Damarin, 1994); caring has also be applied to teacher education (Arnstine, 1990; Rogers & Webb, 1991; Rosiek, 1994) and educational administration (Courtney, 1992; Estes, 1994).

Caring is widely believed to be a central facet of teaching. Kohl, for example, asserts that "a teacher has an obligation to care about every student" (Kohl, 1984, p. 66); Rogers & Webb insist "good teachers care, and good teaching is inextricably linked to specific acts of caring" (Rogers & Webb, 1991, p. 174). By extension, the development of an ethic of care is also seen as a central concern of teacher education (Goodlad, Soder & Sirotnik, 1990) and an important aspect of preservice teachers' field placement experiences (Rogers & Webb, 1991). Noddings writes: "Practice in teaching should be practice in caring. . . [T]here is an attitude to be sustained and enhanced as well as a set of skills to be learned" (Noddings, 1986, p. 504).

Though caring is a term widely used by educators and educational theorists and researchers, the range of meanings attached to "caring" is frequently underexplored and under-discussed. Rogers & Webb exemplify this problem when they state "our knowledge of caring is tacit; it is implicit in action. In other words, although we have difficulty defining it, we know it when we see it" (Rogers & Webb, 1991, p. 177).

To further complicate matters, although there have been attempts in the recent literature to root caring in a theoretical framework, most of these attempts have been fairly superficial—generally taking the shape of cursory, parenthetical references to Noddings (1984) or Gilligan (1982)—and the theories developed by these scholars are rarely explored in depth. Instead, most of these recent works seem rooted in the assumption that everyone knows and agrees upon what is meant by the term caring: one author writes "when we think of caring, we usually think of gentle smiles and warm hugs" (Rogers, 1994, p. 33). The generic, operational definition of caring in classrooms includes images of a teacher being nurturing, supportive, nice, inclusive, responsive, and kind.

My goal in this book is to take steps toward reclaiming caring in teaching and in teacher education. Our conversations must shift away from the "gentle smiles and warm hugs" view of caring toward a view that positions caring as a crucial factor in the teaching-learning process, a powerful intellectual and professional stance for teachers, and a solid foundation upon which to build teacher education programs. I will call this new vision of caring teaching the "moral and intellectual relation" view both to highlight some of its most important features and to foreground the significant ways in which it departs from the currently accepted gentle smiles and warm hugs view.[1]

---

[1] I use the term "gentle smiles and warm hugs" throughout this book as a broad and convenient marker to describe a particular way of thinking about caring. It is a wonderfully vivid and evocative phrase, and I am grateful to Dwight Rogers for capturing that image on paper. Although this is probably self-evident, I feel I must make it clear that Rogers is one of the preeminent scholars exploring the

In Section I, "why care about caring teaching?," I offer conceptual, theoretical and empirical interpretations of caring that provide a framework for the moral and intellectual relation view of caring. This section lays the groundwork for the process of reclaiming caring that is at the heart of this book.

To begin, chapter 1, "Caring in theory and in practice," outlines the current state of conversations about caring in elementary school contexts. In this chapter, I analyze the ways in which the usual discourse around caring—that caring is little more than gentle smiles and warm hugs—is problematic. In place of the usual discourse, I offer Nel Noddings's (1984) work on the ethic of care as the foundation of the moral and intellectual relation view of caring and as the theoretical basis for caring teaching. Drawing on narrative vignettes of daily life in a primary grade classroom, I connect Noddings's philosophical theories directly to elementary teaching practices. The theory helps illuminate the practice and the practice helps clarify the theory; the two work in concert to illustrate the ways in which the moral and intellectual relation view of caring offers teachers a powerful professional stance.

Chapter 2, "Caring and cognitive growth," builds on Noddings's foundation for caring teaching by integrating her work with that of psychologist Lev Vygotsky (1962, 1978). In this chapter, I argue that caring teaching-learning relationships are a prerequisite for intellectual growth. Viewing caring as a relation rather than as a personality trait or a set of friendly behaviors allows us to understand caring as a conscious pedagogical decision and a powerful pedagogical tool.

Section II, "Learning about caring teaching: preservice teachers' perspectives and reflections," builds on the ideas developed in the previous section. Given that the moral and intellectual relation view of caring is a crucial factor in fostering

---

relationships of caring, teaching, and teacher education, and his own beliefs and writings about caring are not at all aligned with the simplistic use I ascribe to the term "gentle smiles and warm hugs" in this book. I hold him and his work in high regard.

children's intellectual growth, we need to educate teachers to understand and to be committed to this vision of caring teaching. One starting place for this complex endeavor is to learn more about the beliefs and understandings of caring that preservice teachers bring to their teacher education experiences and to examine the ways that those preconceptions are challenged during the students' field placement period.

In chapter 3, "Preservice teachers and caring," discussion of the literature on caring in teacher education and description of the empirical work that has been done in the field set the stage for an overview of my recent study of a group of undergraduate elementary teacher education students at a research university in the southern United States. In this chapter, I describe the research design, the setting, the participants, and the methodologies I used in studying the understandings of the role of caring in educational contexts brought by these novices to their first field placement experiences.

In chapter 4, "Initial understandings of caring teaching," I begin to share the results of the study. Rather than attending to process variables—the preservice teachers' emergent practices—I focus upon presage variables—the preservice teachers' beliefs and understandings—and the preservice teachers' reflections on their classroom experiences. Chapter 5, "Challenges enacting caring teaching," follows the preservice teachers into their field placement classrooms, exploring the ways in which their preconceived understandings of caring teaching, described in detail in the previous chapter, played out as they engaged in their first long-term teaching experiences.

In Section III: "Teaching about caring teaching: a teacher educator's perspectives and reflections," I explore possibilities for the development of teacher education programs designed to help preservice teachers come to understand the pedagogical power of the moral and intellectual relation view of caring.

Chapter 6, "Confronting failures in caring," takes a critical turn, calling attention to the ways that caring has become one of the regimes of truth (Gore, 1993) that undergird our current teacher education practices. To do so, I turn a critical eye on my own teacher education practices, examining the ways that, like the preservice teachers in my study, my own ability to understand and enact caring practices was limited and partial. Despite my good intentions, I was unable to reclaim caring within the situation I had constructed for myself and my students in this study; I found that it would not be possible to do so while working within the existing structures of teacher education.

My findings in this study suggest that in order to reclaim caring in teaching and teacher education, a reconceived approach to teacher education is needed. In chapter 7, "Towards a vision of caring teaching: The Cornerstones of Caring model," I draw on the work of Nel Noddings and others to create a new model of teacher education. Called the Cornerstones of Caring, this model emphasizes commitment, community, and passion, and aims to prepare teachers who will be able to draw upon a moral and intellectual relation view of caring to build a strong foundation for their professional practices and who will be able to take advantage of the pedagogical power of caring in their work with children.

SECTION I

WHY CARE ABOUT
CARING TEACHING?

Chapter 1

Caring in Theory and in Practice

The word caring has been overused, poorly defined, and under-theorized in our field because we have allowed it to happen. We have accepted tacit definitions and implied theories, we have assumed shared understanding and mutual agreement. The meanings generally assigned to caring in educational contexts fall under the "gentle smiles and warm hugs" heading: caring teachers are nice, friendly, smiling, loving. Caring teachers give lots of hugs. Caring teachers are endlessly patient, always have time for their students, go the extra mile. Caring is conceived of as a feeling, or a set of feelings, that causes a teacher to behave in a certain way.

While we surely want classrooms that are characterized by warmth, nurturance, inclusion, and support for children, linking these traits to the term caring poses some significant problems for the field of education. Caring has long been considered an essential aspect of teaching children, however, these commonly held definitions and understandings of caring—the "gentle smiles and warm hugs" view (Rogers, 1994, p. 33)—position caring in the affective domain: caring is a feeling, a personality trait, a temperament (Katz, 1971). In this view, caring is not an intellectual act. This understanding of caring limits our conception of what it means to be a teacher and obscures the complexity and the intellectual challenge of the work we do.

To combat this problem, we must take strides toward developing and communicating an understanding of caring that emphasizes its deeply ethical, philosophical, and experiential roots. Feminist moral theory, specifically the ethic of care, can provide such an understanding of caring. The conception of caring emerging from these theories captures the moral and intellectual nature of the teaching profession in ways that the conception of caring drawn from some commonly understood image of nice, friendly teachers hugging kids could never do.

In this chapter, I discuss in some depth the notion of the ethic of care, emphasizing the perspectives developed by Nel Noddings (1984). Noddings's theories form the foundation for the moral and intellectual relation view of caring; one purpose of this chapter is to develop an clear understanding of caring that forms the heart of this new view.

In addition to explicating Noddings's definitions of caring and caring encounters, I link her theories directly to elementary education practices in this chapter. I do this by providing examples of caring-centered teaching drawn from a recent study undertaken in Martha George's primary grade classroom in suburban California (Goldstein, 1997). My intent is to use these narratives of classroom life to highlight the ways that the ethic of care and the moral and intellectual relation view of caring that emerges from it can be used to enhance our understanding of what it means to be caring teachers, and to illustrate the ways that the philosophical and theoretical foundations of the ethic of care can been understood with ease in relation to common teaching-learning interactions. Being a caring teacher in accordance with the moral and intellectual relation view of caring is not difficult or artificial—in this chapter, linking Martha George's work to Noddings's theories highlights the ways that the theories and our practices make sense together. If we are to move caring beyond gentle smiles and warm hugs and beyond its current status as "buzzword of the month" to its rightful place at the heart of teaching and learning, then we must not shy away from its intellectual roots in feminist moral theory. Only by fully understanding caring will we be able to make the most of its pedagogical power in our work with children and with preservice teachers.

The ethic of care

In her landmark book, *In a Different Voice* (1982), Carol Gilligan asserts that women make decisions in ways that enable them to maintain relationships and to sustain connections. This type of reasoning is distinctly different from that implied by traditional moral theory, in which good decisions are made in accordance with universal principles. In her research on women's moral decision making, Gilligan found that abstract principles were fairly irrelevant to the women she studied. Her female participants tended to take contextual factors into account and were neither able nor willing to reduce complex situations to simple black and white.

Gilligan proposed an alternative model of moral development — an ethic of responsibility in contrast to a morality of rights (Gilligan, 1982, p. 164) — and opened the door to further inquiry into the nature of women's ways of thinking about the world and their experiences in it. Her work was followed by a powerful flow of feminist writing on issues in ethics. The authors of these works on what is now known as the ethic of care intended to "develop a feminist moral theory to deal with the regions of experience that have been central to women's experience and neglected by traditional moral theory" (Held, 1987, p. 114).

Though many feminist scholars have explored the nature of care and concern (Belenky, Clinchy, Goldberger & Tarule, 1986; Card, 1990; Collins, 1991; Held, 1987; Hoagland, 1990; Larrabee, 1993; Tronto, 1993), Nel Noddings's work *Caring* (1984) has been the most influential in the field of education. When Noddings uses the term caring, she is describing not an attribute or personality trait, but a moral relation. Caring is not something you are, but rather something you engage in, something you do. Every interaction provides one with an opportunity to enter into a caring relation. Noddings emphasizes the ethic of care's deep moral dimension: "One must meet the other in caring. From this requirement there is no escape for one who would be moral" (Noddings, 1984, p. 201). Caring, then, is simultaneously a choice, a responsibility, and an obligation, involving both affect and volition.

As Noddings describes it, each caring encounter is an interaction between a person giving care and a person receiving that care: a one-caring and a cared-for.[1] In a caring encounter, the one-caring meets the cared-for with engrossment. The one-caring opens herself to the cared-for with full attention, and with receptivity to his perspective and situation. Noddings's understanding of what it means to care is rooted in an extremely specific definition of receptivity, one which departs in important ways from the usual usage: for Noddings, receptivity is not synonymous with empathy. To the contrary, in Noddings's depiction of a caring encounter, the one-caring does not empathize with the cared-for, trying to imagine how she would feel were she in his situation. The one-caring does not project, analyze, or generalize. Instead, as Noddings writes, "I receive the other into myself and I see and feel with the other. I become a duality" (Noddings, 1984, p. 30). The one-caring must engage in "feeling with" the other, attempting, to the greatest degree possible, to feel what he feels.

Receptivity is of central importance in Noddings's conception of caring; the experience of fully receiving the other is the catalyst for the caring encounter. Once the one-caring has received the cared-for, she feels a compelling obligation to respond; in this way, receptivity triggers the caring encounter. Noddings describes this further: "[when] I take on the other's reality as possibility and begin to feel its reality, I feel, also, that I must act accordingly; that is, I am impelled to act as though in my own behalf, but in behalf of the other" (Noddings, 1984, p. 16).

The one-caring's stance is also characterized by motivational displacement, defined by Noddings as the willingness to give

---

[1]For the sake of simplicity and clarity, I shall refer to the one-caring as "she," and the cared-for as "he" throughout this book. Certainly, individuals of either gender can, and should, fill either role. I shall continue this semantic distinction when referring in general to teachers and students as well: the teacher will be "she," the student "he."

primacy, even momentarily, to the goals and needs of the cared-for. Motivational displacement is a direct outcome of receptivity; when the one-caring is feeling with the cared-for, fully receiving him, his motives become her motives. As Noddings puts it, motivational displacement "involves stepping out of one's own personal frame of reference and into the other's" (Noddings, 1984, p. 24). It is not enough simply to respond to the cared-for; the response must be shaped by the process of motivational displacement.

For an interaction to be considered a caring encounter, it is necessary that the one-caring demonstrate both engrossment and motivational displacement. To illustrate: if Student A approached me asking for assistance in resolving his dispute with Student B over the use of the paper cutter in our classroom, my listening closely and fully receiving Student A, feeling and experiencing as closely as possible the parameters of his experience, would be an example of engrossment.

If my response to Student A were to emerge solely out of my own goals and desires—if I were to use this dispute as a long-awaited opportunity to send Student B to the principal's office— then no motivational displacement has occurred, and our interaction could not be characterized as a caring encounter. Motivational displacement requires that my response to Student A emerges from his own needs and goals. If Student A's desire was to solve his dispute without negative social repercussions and to use the paper cutter as he had originally intended, and my response was rooted in those desires and facilitated that outcome, then motivational displacement has occurred and our interaction would fit Noddings's criteria for appropriate behavior for the one-caring in a caring encounter.

In determining the appropriate caring response, the one-caring does not give the cared-for what she would want were she in his situation, but attempts to feel what the cared-for feels in order to discern what he himself would want. The one-caring takes into consideration the other's wants, desires, and goals, which she has apprehended as a result of her receptivity, and reflects upon both his objective needs and what he expects of her. The appropriate caring response, then, is contextually specific, rooted in the particularities of a specific pair of individuals in a concrete situation: "the actions of one-caring will be varied rather than rule-bound; that is, her actions, while predictable in a global sense, will be unpredictable in detail" (Noddings, 1984, p. 24).

The combination of engrossment and motivational displacement can happen on many different levels, from the intense—a mother caring for an infant—to the fleeting—a stranger on campus stopping a busy professor to ask for directions. Though it is easy to envision the mother-infant relation as caring, the second scenario is equally well explained as a caring encounter using Noddings's definitions and terminology. The busy professor pauses, listening carefully to the request of the stranger (Noddings's engrossment). She has temporarily ceased her own musings and given primacy to the pressing needs of the stranger (Noddings's motivational displacement). It is the engrossment and motivational displacement that are the hallmarks of caring, not the depth of feeling. As Noddings explains, "I do not need to establish a deep, lasting, time-consuming personal relationship with every [cared-for]. What I must do is to be totally and nonselectively present to the [cared-for] . . . as he addresses me. The time interval may be brief but the encounter is total" (Noddings, 1984, p. 180).

The caring encounter is completed once the cared-for has acknowledged the care he has received. Reciprocity can take different forms—smiles and gurgles from a baby, a thank you from the lost stranger—but it must occur in every caring encounter. This reciprocity is the sole responsibility of the cared-for in a caring relation. However, it is a very powerful role. The one-caring is dependent on the cared-for—whatever the one-caring does is validated and made meaningful, or diminished and made meaningless, by the response of the cared-for (Noddings, 1984, p. 60-1). The responsiveness of the cared-for can take many different forms, depending on the individuals, the nature of their relationship, and the dimensions of their interaction. Regardless of the form it takes, the cared-for's response is the one-caring's reward, and is the impetus for her continued caring. Noddings (1984, p. 52) reflects on this dimension of her own experience as one-caring:

> I am aided in meeting the burdens of caring by the reciprocal efforts of the cared-for. When my infant wriggles with delight as I bathe or feed him, I am aware of no burden but only a special delight of my own. Similarly, when I spend time in dialogue with my students, I am rewarded not only with appreciation, but also with all sorts of information and insights. I could as easily, and properly, say "I am receiving" as "I am giving." Thus, many of the "demands" of caring are not felt as demands. They are, rather, the occasions that offer most of what makes life worth living.

In Noddings's view, caring is not a stance that can be adopted and discarded at will. Meeting others as one-caring is the "first and unending obligation" (Noddings, 1984, p. 17) of those who wish to be moral. It is a deliberate, conscious choice, and an ethical ideal. Noddings (1984, p. 84) writes, "The source of my obligation is the value I place on the relatedness of caring. This value itself arises as a product of actual caring and being cared-for and my reflection on the goodness of these concrete caring situations." By extension, this moral imperative to meet others as one-caring is pervasive, moving beyond one's inner circle and reaching out into all aspects of life.

In mature, healthy relationships, all involved parties get the opportunity to be both the one-caring and the cared-for. The mother-infant relationship, on the other hand, is bound to be very one-sided: the mother is always the one-caring and the infant always the cared-for. Yet their caring encounters are mutually satisfying. Noddings (1992, p. 17) writes:

> In every caring encounter the mother is necessarily carer and the infant cared-for. But the infant responds—he or she coos, wriggles, stares attentively, smiles, reaches out, and cuddles. These responses are heartwarming; they make caregiving a rewarding experience.

These caring encounters are also learning experiences for the infant. It is by being the cared-for that he or she will learn how to be one-caring.

This detail has significant implications for schooling. Teachers who meet their students as ones-caring and who look upon the act of teaching as an opportunity to participate in caring encounters will be teaching their students more than academic knowledge. These children will have the opportunity to learn how to care. This moves beyond the mere modeling of desired behaviors. It is a moral stance that has the potential to transform education.

The ethic of care provides a way of thinking about caring that repositions the concept, transforming it from a personality trait to a deliberate and decisive act. Thinking about teacherly caring using Noddings's work as a conceptual framework enables us to understand more fully the intellectual aspects of caring, and allows us to think of caring as a sound foundation for teaching practices and decision making. Noddings's ideas transform the gentle smiles and warm hugs view of caring into the moral and intellectual relation view of caring.

That caring, as Noddings describes it, arises out of lived experience with caring relationships suggests that many teachers are already likely to be active practitioners of the "moral and intellectual relation" type of caring. Our experiences in classrooms with children have shaped and informed our understandings of teaching and learning. Without our knowing it, Noddings's theories are reflected in our practices, and our practices echo in her theories.

Enacting the ethic of care

To illustrate the relationships between Noddings's theories and the practices of caring teaching, I will apply her definition of caring—an encounter between a one-caring and a cared-for characterized by engrossment and motivational displacement on the part of the one-caring and reciprocity on the part of the cared-for—to the interpretation of the teaching practices of Martha

George, a teacher in a multiage kindergarten/first/second grade class in a suburban California elementary school. I spent over 150 hours as a participant observer in Martha's classroom during a three-month period in 1994 to explore the ways that love and care impacted her teaching practices and my own (Goldstein, 1997).

My purpose in sharing these stories here is neither to determine whether or not Martha George is a caring teacher nor to prove that Noddings's definition of caring is correct and accurate. Rather, I intend to use Martha's teaching to provide concrete examples of the ways that Noddings's theories about the ethic of care can be used to enrich our understanding of the teaching decisions, practices, and interactions common to many elementary school classroom contexts.

Noddings asserts that "caring is a way of being in relation, not a set of specific behaviors" (Noddings, 1992, p. 17). However, she does point to engrossment and motivational displacement as behavioral indicators of caring and also provides the following guidelines to assist observers in identifying caring encounters (Noddings, 1984, p. 24-5):

> The observer. . . cannot see the crucial motive and may misread the attitudinal signs. The observer, then, must judge caring, in part, by the following: First, the action . . . either brings about a favorable outcome for the cared-for or seems reasonably likely to do so; second, the one-caring displays a characteristic variability in her actions—she acts in a nonrule-bound fashion in behalf of the cared-for.

Drawing on these guidelines in my observations and analyses of Martha's caring teaching practices, I looked for evidence of engrossment and receptivity, motivational displacement, variability in response to the needs of individual students, and indications that her actions were intended to lead to a favorable outcome for her students.

Martha George's work day begins long before her students arrive at school. She readies her classroom while the morning sky is still dark. Though it starts with just a trickle, a steady stream of minivans and Volvo station wagons soon floods the Bayview Elementary School parking lot, and the sounds of children fill the air. There are no bells to wait for: Martha's students kiss their moms good-bye and charge straight into their classroom, dragging their backpacks, lunch boxes, and other accouterments of childhood. They all seem to know just what to do. They unpack their belongings, turn over their attendance cards, put lunch tickets into the special canister. The children do not have their own desks, as they might in some elementary school classrooms, so special treasures—little hair barrettes, baseball cards, geodes, plastic doodads of all kinds—are secreted away into cubbies to be retrieved at recess.

Martha perches on a tiny child-sized chair on the open patch of carpet at the side of the room. She talks and jokes with the children who gather around her. Several children lie on the rug reading books, others sit on the unsightly brown plaid sofa. Every so often Martha breaks away from her conversation to redirect a child who has gotten too boisterous: "Connor, do you remember what you are supposed to be doing right now?," she asks gently.

She begins each day the same way, with meeting. "Okay! Please put your books away and come over to the rug to hear the lunch choices," she says. Even the children who are not buying lunch come over excitedly: they know that listening carefully to the lunch count will pay off. Martha continues, "The choices for today are baked chicken, wild pizza, sub sandwich, nachos, or hamburger." Martha stops what she is doing and turns to look at a wiggling, giggling boy with shiny black hair. "Andy...," she says quietly. Andy busily pokes at the boy sitting beside him, unaware that he is the focus of the teacher's attention. Martha tries again, a bit louder this time. "Andy." He looks up at her sheepishly and puts his hands in his lap. "Andy, you're going to want to listen carefully to this so that you can make a good decision about lunch." Martha does not scold or reprimand. Andy simply needs to listen so that he can make a good choice. Martha continues the lunch count, marking the children's choices on the attendance clipboard.

The lunch count is then transformed into a math problem: "One person ordered chicken, three people ordered pizza, zero people ordered the submarine sandwich, two people ordered nachos, and one person ordered a hamburger. How many lunches is that all together?" Martha asks the class. As she reads off the tally, the children count on their fingers, keeping track of the total. "If you think that you have the answer, hold up that number of fingers and show it to a friend," Martha says. The children wave their hands wildly, fingers outstretched. Most hold up seven, a few hold eight or six. Some of the younger children look around quickly and put up the same number of fingers as their neighbor; others simply put both hands in the air and wiggle all of their fingers. Martha continues the routine. "When I count to three, you can call out your answer. 1 . . . 2 . . . 3!" The room echoes with the sound of children joyfully calling out "SEVEN!!!" "Oh, I heard a lot of sevens, that's great," concludes Martha. The children squirm with joy and pull down their clenched fists, hissing "yesssss!" as if they had just hit the lottery jackpot. Even those children who yelled out "SIX" or "EIGHT" were excited — they had meant to say seven, after all.

Meeting continues. While Martha's attention is momentarily focused on Mitchell's whispered commentary to his neighbor, Gus, a very small boy with translucent white skin who is clearly a kindergartner, raises his hand and calls out, "Martha? Connor is bothering me . . ." He looks indignant, clearly The Wronged Party, and waits smugly for Martha to have a few words with Connor. Martha looks at Gus and whispers her response as she gropes for the orange marker beneath her chair. "Do you know who you need to talk to about that?" she asks. Gus seems unsure, and thinks for a moment, brow furrowed. It is likely that in his previous school experiences, or at playdates, or in the park, an adult has been summoned to settle disputes and smooth ruffled feathers. "A grown-up?" he suggests. Martha shakes her head and replies, "I think that you can talk to Connor about that." The students need to solve their own problems, make their own choices, and learn to take responsibility for their own behavior.

As Martha steps over to the calendar, she asks Mitchell to move away from Mark. She issues her request in a whisper, as if misbehavers do not deserve her full voice. Like the lunch count, the calendar routine is suffused with mathematical concepts: odd and even numbers, patterning, place value, graphing. Mitchell does not move and continues to disturb Mark and some of the other children around him. Martha whirls around, marker poised in midair. She gives Mitchell a stern look, and says firmly, "Mitchell, if you want to choose a new spot for yourself, you will have to do it now. If you don't, I'll choose for you." Mitchell wants to choose for himself; he wants to make a good decision. He stands, moves away from Mark, and finds a new spot, turning around like a puppy several times before sitting down.

In Noddings's conception of caring, emphasis is given to motivational displacement: the one-caring must give primacy to the needs and goals of the cared-for. Weight is also given to the idea that a caring encounter is characterized by indications that a one-caring's actions were intended to lead to a favorable outcome for her students. Martha's interactions with two of her misbehaving students during this morning's meeting highlight the tension between these two facets of caring. Noddings, too, acknowledges this complexity. She points out "we cannot always act in ways which bring immediate reactions of pleasure from our children" (Noddings, 1984, p. 24).

Though Martha conceives of routine forms of classroom management as opportunities to engage in caring encounters, there are times when she is not willing to give primacy to the students' desires and goals. In this particular case, she does not allow Andy or Mitchell to disturb their classmates during meeting. In fact, she goes so far as to insist that Mitchell relinquish his chosen spot on the carpet to ensure that the disruptions cease. Martha makes these specific pedagogical and managerial choices because she believes that the academic and social content of the class's morning meeting is more important and more valuable to Andy and Mitchell than their desire to wiggle, giggle, and fidget. In this particular caring encounter, Martha's level of motivational displacement is low, however, her decisions are clearly driven by her desire for her students to learn and to grow. Caring encounters, then, are variable in their composition and contours.

In a statement that accurately describes Martha's morning meeting, Noddings states: "Conflict may arise between . . . what the cared-for wants and what we see as his best interest" (Noddings, 1984, p. 55). This issue is of particular relevance in primary grade settings. Because of the young age and concomitant levels of foresight and judgment of the students, primary teachers are regularly confronted by the reality that a child's immediate personal goals might be inappropriate (chatting during meeting), unacceptable (stealing from a classmate), or unsafe (running with scissors). Teachers surely have an obligation to foster the growth of their students (Dewey, 1938; Noddings, 1984; Ruddick, 1989), but the precise balance between teacher choice and child choice is unclear. A teacher's response must be situated, and contextually specific.

In asserting the central role of Dewey's belief that "what the best and wisest parent wants for his own child, that must the community want for all of its children" (Dewey, 1902/1990, p. 7) in her vision of caring education, Noddings gives the adult, the one-caring, a great deal of responsibility for determining the appropriate goals for the cared-fors. This does not allow the one-caring free reign, however. Noddings (1984, p. 23) points out:

> When we care, we should, ideally, be able to present reasons for our action/inaction which would persuade a reasonable, disinterested observer that we have acted in behalf of the cared-for. This does not mean that all such observers have to agree that they would have behaved exactly as we did in a particular caring situation . . . . [But] the reasons we give . . . should be so well connected to the objective elements of the problem that our course of action clearly either stands a chance of succeeding in behalf of the cared-for, or can have been engaged in only with the hope of effecting something for the cared-for.

Though Andy and Mitchell were very interested in their own agendas during this morning's meeting, Martha did not feel that their desire to squirm and chat were in their best interests, either educationally or socially. Her course of action — asking Andy to be still, insisting that Mitchell find a new location on the carpet—arose from her plan to provide them with educative experiences. Martha arrived at a solution that worked well in the specific context of her classroom, her students, and her personal working understanding of caring teaching practices.

Activity time

Martha plans five different activities for each day, all of which go on simultaneously at different locations in the room. On any given day there is an assortment of adults in the room—Martha's aide Yvette, a variety of tutors employed by the district, parent volunteers—and each activity is generally supervised by an adult. Once the children have finished their work, they are welcome to read, write in their journals, work on some ongoing mathematics projects, or have free choice, which includes playing with blocks, Legos or puzzles, doing small-scale art projects, playing in the house area, working with clay.

Martha describes each of the activities to the children during meeting. When activity time begins, the children will go to a station that Martha has selected for them. Placements are made very deliberately. Martha pays close and sensitive attention to the children as individuals, enacting Noddings's notion of engrossment. She explains her decision making process:

> It depends on what [activities] I've got out and who I think will work together well or not. And sometimes it's more because I've seen certain kids have an interest in each other and I'll pair them together. Sometimes I try to structure it so that there's a real heterogeneous group in terms of kids who will be able to help each other, kids who are going to need support functioning at that station. And I also try to somewhat balance it for boys and girls. I try to encourage kids who I think would not try certain things . . . to try everything, to go everywhere.

The children sitting on the rug at Martha's feet do not know about how carefully their needs, personalities, and desires are taken into consideration when these decisions are made. They just know that Martha has a tiny square of paper with the class list printed on it that tells who goes where, and that almost every morning meeting ends with Martha searching for her misplaced list. She finds it quickly this morning, and the children lean forward, eager to hear where they will be sent. Some even have their fingers crossed for good luck, hoping to be sent to the activity of their choice.

It seems odd that 5, 6, and 7 year old children are not given the opportunity to make their own choices at this juncture. In assigning children to activity centers, it seems that Martha has bypassed motivational displacement, a necessary feature of a caring encounter as described by Noddings. It appears Martha is favoring traditional teacher-directed practices over helping the children in her care to determine and attain their own goals. But closer analysis reveals that this particular facet of Martha's practice is actually the outcome of several careful and deliberate decisions linked to Martha's own understanding and interpretation of the principles of caring educational practices.

Martha believes the issues brought to the fore in her discussion of her placement guidelines—giving children opportunities to make interpersonal connections, cooperation and peer teaching, gender equity, risk taking—are crucial. So crucial, in fact, that she is willing to elevate this particular set of objectives over the objective of child choice. In making care-centered pedagogical and curricular decisions, Martha must evaluate her goals for her students, assess her priorities, and balance conflicting demands, all while taking into consideration the context and the needs of the individual students. Her commitment to being responsive to the individuals in her classroom are of primary importance in this particular instance.

Martha begins the morning's placements. "At the round table," she says, pointing, "kids will be working on making their solar system puzzles. They need to be colored, glued, and then cut, just like I showed you. It needs to happen in that order, or else it will get very tricky." She reads the names of the children going to that station.

As the solar system puzzle-makers leave the meeting area and settle down at their table, Martha dismisses the other children to their stations. Some will be making samples of Mars soil with sand, steel wool, and water. Some will be writing in their journals about the Mars lander spacecrafts they built during activity time yesterday. Others will be doing an activity with pattern blocks.

Martha introduces the last activity of the morning to the children who remain on the rug. "At the zigzag table," Martha continues, "Moon reports. Olders need to look in the books on the table and find three facts about the moon that you would like to include in your report. Youngers may pick up one of the sheets that I made and trace the words." She reads off the names, but does not specify who is an older and who is a younger. Second graders are olders, kindergartners are youngers, for certain. But where do the first graders fit? I asked Martha about this, and she replied:

> It depends. It is not cut and dried at all and it varies from situation to situation. I usually leave it up to the kids to decide (trails off). Well, that's not entirely true either. I expect the second graders to do the more demanding option, and they know that. And I assume that most of the kinders will choose the simpler option. Though sometimes they surprise me, like Brian or Robert will choose to do the olders' page. And that's fine. The first graders tend to (pause) well, some of the first graders, like Lauren or Eleanor, are very capable academically, and they'll always opt to do the harder page. And some of the first graders who are just getting started with their writing skills, like Li Ping, for example, will take the easier page, and that's okay. And there are some first graders who are capable but who don't want to put forth much effort . . . they do the easier page too. And though that is not what I'd want for them academically, it tells me something about where they are at in other areas of their development. Sometimes I'll push those kids, and sometimes I won't. It depends.

Martha's personal understanding of caring teaching is prominently featured in this passage. The parallels to Noddings's characteristics of a caring encounter—engrossment, motivational displacement, variability in expectations and responses, actions intended to lead to a favorable outcome for the cared-fors—are also easily visible. Martha provides a range of tasks suited to a variety of ability levels. She is flexible and responsive to each child as an individual, and structures the activities in ways that allow the children to work at their appropriate level. She uses the anecdotal evidence generated by her observations of the children in this situation as a form of assessment. She gives primacy to the children's own desires and goals for themselves. Further, she considers the choices that the children make in this situation to be significant and revealing: they are sources of information with implications for understanding the children's academic and personal development. Her statement "it depends," repeated twice in this passage, captures the fluidity of her decision making and reveals the importance of contextual factors in her practice.

As Noddings's work on caring would demand, Martha's approach to teaching is fundamentally rooted in a commitment to each child as an individual. Martha wrote in our dialogue journal: "It is very important to me that I respond to each child as an individual, which means really knowing them, which means investing in them emotionally." Responding to children as individuals is one of the fundamental tenets of progressive education (Dewey, 1938) and of high quality primary grade education (Bredekamp & Copple, 1997). However, Martha takes this one step further. She is not content to stop at "really knowing them" in order to respond to their individual needs, but she also requires "investing in them emotionally" in order to do this type of work. This emotional investment, perhaps one of the deepest forms of engrossment, is one significant way that caring manifests itself and plays a role in Martha's life as a teacher. She not only thinks carefully about each child, but also cares deeply about each child, and about each child's experience in the classroom.

In describing the role of the one-caring in planning curriculum and instruction, Noddings writes: "the one-caring . . . watches for incipient interest in the child—the particular, concrete child—and arranges the educational environment accordingly" (Noddings, 1984, p. 63). This is indeed the case with Martha's planning strategy. As she wrote in our dialogue journal:

This is not something I think about explicitly for every activity I choose, but I think that love guides my overall choices. I want activities that the kids will love and remember, activities that will stretch them to find out something not just about the activities but about themselves as well. More specifically, love influences my decisions because I connect what I know about each child as an individual with what activities they would particularly connect with or enjoy. I think about who will be really good at an activity and gain emotionally from that and/or share their success with the others.

Giving her full attention to the needs, strengths, and desires of her cared-fors, and balancing those with her own goals for each of the children (Dewey, 1938), Martha plans educational experiences in a way that will lead not only to increased knowledge but also to emotional growth.

Curriculum and lesson planning follow the same line of reasoning as placement at activity centers: Martha's attentive focus on each child as an individual and her own strategies for balancing the tension between teacher goals and student desires allow her to feel comfortable making these kinds of judgment calls on her own, without much direct input from the children. Martha is committed to allowing children to play an active role in directing their own learning, but only to a certain point.

Martha appreciates the importance of child choice but does not provide it in all ways or at all times. In some instances, motivational displacement takes precedence, and Martha elevates the children's goals over her own. In other instances, Martha's own sense of the children's best interests eclipses the children's personally-held desires. Far from being problematic, this inconsistency is the hallmark of caring practice: as Noddings points out, ones-caring act in a nonrule-bound manner in behalf of their cared-fors (Noddings, 1984, p. 24-5).

Recognizing that "enormous variance exists in the timing of individual development that is within the normal range" (Bredekamp, 1987, p. 65), Martha feels comfortable letting go of rigid expectations for coverage of material. Instead, she attempts to cover the broad spectrum of her children's needs and abilities and focuses on growth rather than approximation of pre-determined end-points. As she said:

> I have to take it sort of from where they come in at to what they're next able to (pause) like, obviously, my goals in terms of Connor being able to interact appropriately with other children and enter social groups and aid somebody else are based on improving from wherever he started at. So my ultimate ending expectation for him might be different than for someone like Lauren who had strong pro-social skills when she came in.

Martha's approach illustrates well Noddings's assertion that "caring teachers will . . . respond differentially to their students" (Noddings, 1992, p. 19). This attitude is also apparent in some of Martha's assessment procedures. For example, she asked the children to do some cutting with scissors at the start of the year. "I had all the kids cut along certain lines for me at the beginning of the year — a straight, a zig-zag, a curve — to see where their cutting was at. I am looking for a big, long-term thing about how their cutting has changed over the course of the year in here." Children's progress will be evaluated in terms of the distance traveled from their personal starting point, rather than in terms of their ability to reach a predetermined, external standard.

Acknowledging and responding to individual differences is a central part of Nel Noddings's vision of caring education. In *The Challenge to Care in Schools* (Noddings, 1992), Noddings suggests that no one should be required to take algebra, or a foreign language, or creative writing: each child's education should be tailored to his or her capabilities, interests, desire and goals. Noddings's plans for a curriculum centered around domains of care, developed in response to her concerns about the disconnected and disjointed structure of the secondary school educational experience, evoke the thematic organization and student-centered atmosphere of classrooms like Martha's. In fact, Noddings states that: "some of the best planning for curriculum and instruction that I have observed has been at the nursery-kindergarten level" (Noddings, 1992, p. 175). Nel Noddings and Martha George share an interest in operationalizing the ethic of care in their classrooms, and believe in putting students and their needs before all other concerns.

Sometimes Martha's commitment to the children's goals and desires leads to the failure of an activity or lesson. If the children don't buy into a particular idea — making family banners, singing "Parents Are People," writing outer space dictionaries — the activity dies a lonely death, unmourned by the children or their teacher. Noddings asserts that "the student is infinitely more important than the subject" (Noddings, 1984, p. 20): in Martha's classroom the student is infinitely more important than the skill or the activity.

This willingness to let go of her own plans is another example of Martha's enactment of Noddings's notion of motivational displacement. Martha says:

> I don't feel so great as a teacher when I realize that I have a lot invested in a plan, and that it has become more important to me than what [the children] choose to do with it. . . . When [the lesson] doesn't come to fruition the way that I had expected, I like to be able to let go of what I expected, and to let them do with it whatever they need to do with it.

Martha expends a lot of energy in the early stages of each lesson — planning, developing materials, arranging the environment — in order to build a firm foundation for the children's experience with the activity. Once the children begin to interact with the materials, the activity is out of her hands: its success or failure rests with the children. This is one of the ways that Martha balances teacher responsibility and children's desires — the competing interests of the one-caring and the cared-fors.

In one of our long conversations about our teaching practices, Martha described her teaching as a braid of four intertwined strands: "The children, me, the environment, and my philosophy." It is not surprising that Martha started her list with the children. They are the center of the universe she has created in Room 4, and all that occurs in the classroom is in direct response to the children and their needs. Martha's relationships with the children are the most important part of her teaching experience. She said:

> I need that connection to them . . . . It is an interaction that goes back and forth . . . . They know how I feel about them, and they in turn can give that to me. And then, because they give it to me, I can give it back to them . . . . I think that it influences my level of excitement at being with them. It influences me in terms of I want to pick things that they'll love because I want them to love whatever is going on in my class. I think it makes me very thoughtful about things.

This statement touches upon Noddings's notion of reciprocity as the sole role of the cared-for in a caring encounter. Martha's students, her cared-fors, acknowledge the care they receive from their teacher, and do so in ways that deepen and enrich Martha's commitment to meeting them as one-caring. Martha's relationships with the children drive her practice, form the core of her approach to classroom management and organization, and shape her curricular decision making. Teaching is more than a job for Martha. Teaching is a relation.

Despite the obvious emotional depth of Martha's teaching relationships, her practice is not demonstrably loving. Like Martha herself, her care-centered teaching is not effusive, lovey-dovey, or sickly sweet. Martha insists that the children in her care take responsibility for themselves and their own experience: she values and encourages independence, not dependence. She is not an over-bearing carer, clinging tightly to the children and smothering them with her attention. Martha says "I try to communicate [my caring feelings] in lots of subtle ways . . . . I'm not an emotionally flowery person, so I don't do lots of real big shows of affection."

Naturally, an approach to teaching that is so deeply personal is bound to be unique and idiosyncratic: another teacher operationalizing the ethic of care in her work with children is likely to have a care-centered approach to teaching that departs from Martha's in certain aspects. While the essential and critical fundamentals of high-quality education are certainly non-negotiable, cookie-cutter conformity to rule or principle is not in keeping with this perspective on teaching. Though engrossment, motivational displacement and reciprocity are to be expected in a caring teaching environment, the ways that they surface and play out is open to a wide range of possibilities.

As this discussion of Martha George's ethic of care-centered teaching illustrates, the feminist interpretation of caring emerging from the work of Nel Noddings — caring as an action rather than an attribute, and as a deliberate moral and intellectual stance rather than simply a feeling — offers a powerful alternative to the vague and general conceptions of caring currently shaping our conversations about the term. Noddings's vision of caring is a construct which will allow teachers to position caring in a way that offers us the opportunity to enhance and to deepen our understanding of the work we do, and which will provide a strong, powerful alternative to the commonly held sense of caring as little more than those gentle smiles and warm hugs.

Caring teaching is deliberate, thoughtful, responsive, demanding, intellectual, and nuanced, and calls for judgment, sensitivity, flexibility and agility. The gentle smiles and warm hugs view of caring fails to capture these aspects of our work. Using Noddings's definition of caring as a foundation for a different view of teacherly caring, a view that represents caring as a moral and intellectual relation, repositions caring in a way that turns being a caring teacher into a powerful professional stance.

Chapter 2

Caring and Cognitive Growth

In Noddings's perspective, every interaction offers us the opportunity to enter into a caring relation (Noddings, 1984). When we build on this view, caring teaching is no longer understood simply as the tendency to give gentle smiles and warm hugs; instead, caring becomes a way for teachers to make thoughtful professional choices about their interactions with their students. Viewing caring as a moral and intellectual relation provides us with a much needed opportunity to reposition caring in teaching. Emphasizing the relational nature of caring also offers us new insights into the powerful contributions caring makes to teaching-learning interactions. In this chapter, I argue that caring, when seen as a moral and intellectual relation rather than as gentle smiles and warm hugs, is a prerequisite for intellectual growth. Seeing caring as a relation makes this argument possible.

Noddings's description of a caring encounter, described in detail in chapter 1, has remarkably close parallels to Vygotskyan constructs such as intersubjectivity, guided participation, scaffolding and the like. Though Noddings's work and Vygotsky's work are rooted in different disciplines—philosophy and psychology, respectively—they share essential understandings of the contours of the relationship between teacher and learner.

Exploring these similarities reveals new dimensions of teaching, learning, and caring. For example, although constructs such as the co-construction of knowledge and the zone of proximal development originally articulated in Vygotsky's works (1962, 1978) have transformed current thinking in the field of educational psychology, many have criticized Vygotsky's work for its lack of attention to emotion and affect (Newman & Holzman, 1993; Rogoff, 1990). This is a serious shortcoming that prevents Vygotsky's work from being as fully useful as it might be. Drawing on Noddings's work gives us language with which to talk about the affective and volitional dimensions of the zone of proximal development. This broadens the ways in which Vygotsky's work can be used in educational contexts.

Noddings's work is already directly relevant to educational contexts. However, connecting her ideas with those of Vygotsky highlights the fundamental importance of caring relationships in the teaching-learning process and, therefore, in children's cognitive growth. Both Noddings and Vygotsky showcase the vital role of relationship in human life; merging the ethic of care and the notion of the co-construction of knowledge broadens and enriches our conception of the teaching-learning process and enhances our understanding of the roles played by affect, volition, and relationship in cognitive development.

In this chapter, I describe in detail some key features of Vygotsky's work as well as the interpretations of his writing offered by his most influential followers. I elaborate on the relational, affective aspects of the zone of proximal development that have not been explored elsewhere, and I use Noddings's terminology and ideas of a caring encounter to describe the relational face of the zone of proximal development. My goal is to foreground the pedagogical power of caring and to showcase the ways that the moral and intellectual relation view of caring makes access to this power possible.

Elements of the zone

Lev Vygotsky's (1978) assertion that cognitive development is embedded in the context of social relationships has become a widely held belief (Lave & Wenger, 1991; Newman, Griffin & Cole, 1989; Rogoff, 1990; Wertsch, 1985). In this view of cognition, interaction with others is the crucible of intellectual development: as Barbara Rogoff writes, "understanding happens *between* people; it can't be attributed to one individual or the other" (Rogoff, 1990, p. 67). This suggests that the process of cognitive growth is inherently relational. The very notion of the *co-construction* of mind implies a high degree of interpersonal connection between the individuals working together in the process. This emphasis on meaningful interpersonal interaction could imply that affective factors play a central role in intellectual growth and development (Dean, 1994). However, the literature has focused on the more strictly cognitive aspects of the process, leaving the affective nature of teaching-learning interactions unexplored.

The emphasis on intellect at the expense of affect that has characterized recent interpretations and applications of Vygotsky's theories (Berk & Winsler, 1995; Dean, 1994; Packer, 1993; Stone, 1993) is in direct contradiction to Vygotsky's own views on the matter (Newman & Holzman, 1993; Wertsch, 1985). Vygotsky wrote:

> The separation of the intellectual side of our consciousness from its affective, volitional side is one of the fundamental flaws of all of traditional psychology. Because of it thinking is inevitably transformed into an autonomous flow of thoughts thinking themselves. It is separated from all the fullness of real life, from the living motives, interests, and attractions of the thinking human (Vygotsky, cited in Wertsch, 1985, p. 189).

Vygotsky clearly understood the essential role of affect in intellectual experience.[1] In this chapter, I will be echoing and responding to Vygotsky's desire for a seamless union of the cognitive factors and the affective and volitional factors of intellectual life, a union in which affect and volition remain visible and present and not eclipsed by cognition, as has been the case in most other writings on the topic.

---

[1]Making a distinction between cognition and affect is problematic: there is no thinking without feeling nor feeling without thought. However, without making this distinction it would be impossible to clarify which aspects of interpersonal interaction in the zone of proximal development have been well developed and which have been overlooked. This issue became a central dilemma in the writing of this chapter. I have elected to live with this artificial cognitive/affective split in the service of my argument.

Vygotsky (1978, p. 57) saw the process of learning as socially mediated:

> Every function in the child's cultural development appears twice: first, on the social level, and later, on the individual level; first *between* people (*interpsychological*), and then *inside* the child (*intrapsychological*). This applies equally to voluntary attention, to logical memory, and to the formation of concepts. All the higher functions originate as actual relations between human individuals.

As Wertsch (1991, p. 90) puts it, for Vygotsky, "the mind extends beyond the skin" into a socially shared space. Human thought, then, must always be considered within the context of the specific cultural and social contexts in which it occurs. The development of children's higher mental processes is directly shaped both by the knowledge systems, tools, structures, and practices of the socio-cultural milieu in which they are learning and growing, and by the immediate interactions occurring in their zone of proximal development (ZPD), the interpersonal space where learning and development takes place (Berk & Winsler, 1995; Martin, 1990; Moll, 1990; Moll & Greenberg, 1990).

Vygotsky defines the zone of proximal development as "the distance between the actual developmental level as determined by independent problem solving and the level of potential development as determined through problem solving under adult guidance or in collaboration with more capable peers" (1978, p. 86). This particular definition's emphasis on the ZPD as a socially mediated space—a learner's level of assisted performance, one boundary of the zone, is set with "adult guidance or in collaboration with more capable peers"—suggests that the ZPD is formed through relationship.[2]

---

[2]This definition of the zone of proximal development, focused on the guided assistance of a learner by an adult teacher or more capable peer, is one widely researched and discussed aspect of Vygotsky's work, and will be the central focus of this chapter. However, this type of one-on-one interaction is not the only route to the creation of zones of proximal development. Play, for example, allows children to scaffold themselves and create a zone of proximal development without the direct assistance of others (Bodrova & Leong, 1996). Similarly,

The boundaries of the zone—determined by the child's level of independent performance and the child's level of assisted performance—are personal, flexible, and constantly changing. The teacher and the learner interact to create the zone through a process known as intersubjectivity (Newson & Newson, 1975): each participant begins any given task with different understandings of the task, and through a process of negotiation, conversation, compromise, and shared experience, each comes to a new, mutually-held understanding. Rogoff (1986, pp. 32-33) writes:

> In order to communicate successfully, the adult and child must find a common ground of knowledge and skills. Otherwise the two people would be unable to share a common reference point, and understanding would not occur. This effort toward understanding . . . draws the child into a model of the problem that is more mature yet understandable through links with what the child already knows.

In addition to finding a common ground, both the adult and the child are required to change and adjust their understanding of the task during the intersubjective work of establishing a shared intellectual space (Forman, 1989, p. 67). Again, the centrality of interpersonal relationships is readily apparent: the teacher and the student must connect with each other in order to work together productively and successfully.

Newman, Griffin & Cole (1989) have drawn upon the metaphor of a construction zone to describe the zone of proximal development: the ZPD is a site for the co-construction of knowledge. This construction metaphor can be extended and developed further by including the notion of scaffolding, described by Wood, Bruner & Ross (1976, p. 98): the teacher's role is to ensure that a task falls within the child's zone of proximal development, and then to provide temporary, adjustable scaffolding for the child, decreasing the amount of support and

---

children can scaffold themselves through the use of internalized private speech (Berk & Winsler, 1995). Materials such as videos and books can also serve to mediate and create zones of proximal development for children (Martin, 1990).

assistance given as the child becomes increasingly able to perform independently. In addition to the relational process of achieving a level of intersubjectivity, I contend that both the adult and the child must be willing to maintain, support, and transform their learning relationship as the landscape of the ZPD changes. The process of scaffolding positions collaborative relationship as a direct source of cognitive growth.

The interrelational dimension

Vygotsky described work in the ZPD as a "unique form of cooperation between the child and the adult that is the central element of the educational process" (1978, p. 169). Many scholars have endeavored to describe this particular form of cooperation, exploring the ways it takes shape in different contexts and academic disciplines (Forman, 1989; Gonçu, 1993; Moll & Whitmore, 1993; Palincsar, Brown & Campione, 1993; Rogoff, Malkin & Gilbride, 1984; Wertsch, 1979; Wood, Bruner & Ross, 1976; Wood & Middleton, 1975). One result of these studies is a fairly clear picture of what adults do when supporting a child's learning in the zone of proximal development.

Wood, Bruner & Ross (1976, p. 98) found that teachers engage in the following activities while scaffolding their students: recruitment of the child's interest, reduction in degrees of freedom, direction maintenance, marking of critical features in the task, frustration control, and demonstration of idealized solutions. Similarly, Tharp (1993) lists modeling, feedback, contingency management, instructing, questioning, cognitive structuring, and task structuring as effective means of assisting student performance.

Palincsar, Brown & Campione (1993, p. 45) observed teachers successfully supporting their students during literacy instruction by linking students' previous contributions to new knowledge arising in the text, requesting that students elaborate on their ideas, restoring direction to the discussion, and reworking students' contributions so they are integrated into the discussion. Moll & Whitmore (1993) ascribe to the teacher the roles of guide and supporter, active participant, evaluator, and facilitator.

When Rogoff, Malkin & Gilbride (1984, p. 33) discuss the specific nature of what adults do in the zone of proximal development, they write: "The adult emphasizes crucial actions, provides guidance at choice points, and indicates important alternatives in the solution of the problem at hand. The child's state of understanding and contribution to the activity further tailor the interaction to the specific teaching-learning situation." This description highlights the active role of the child in co-creating the zone.

These interpersonal features of the zone of proximal development have been the focus of a great deal of attention, researched in the contexts of mother-child dyads (Rogoff, 1990), teacher-student pairs (Wood, Bruner & Ross, 1976), and peer collaborations (Forman, 1989). I argue that what occurs on this interpersonal plane can be further teased apart, separated into two parallel and simultaneously occurring dimensions: the interpsychological dimension and the interrelational dimension.

The studies cited earlier have attended to the strategies and procedures occurring on what Vygotsky called the interpsychological level, a shared intellectual space created by the adult and child in the ZPD. Just as these strategies and procedures — modeling, feedback, and so on — are situated within and shaped by particular social and cultural contexts, they are also enmeshed with and influenced by features located on what I shall call the interrelational level.

Analogous to the interpsychological dimension, the interrelational dimension is a shared affective space created by the adult and child in the ZPD. The interrelational aspect of the teaching-learning relationship begins before any strategies can be chosen or developed. The interrelational dimension facilitates entry into the zone of proximal development, continues during the pair's experience in the zone, and emerges after the learning experience in a transformed and deepened form.

The literature on the social construction of knowledge in the zone of proximal development has emphasized the interpsychological dimension at the expense of the interrelational. Accounts of the intersubjective aspects of the zone of proximal development generally fail to afford any attention to the affective, relational side of the interpersonal process of negotiating meaning. Though Berk & Winsler hint at the central importance of interpersonal relationship in their suggestion that teachers must "be sensitive to the knowledge, abilities, interests, attitudes, and cultural values and practices that children bring to learning situations" (Berk & Winsler, 1994, p. 131), this idea is not developed into a fully articulated description of the interpersonal, affective features and character of this "unique form of cooperation between the child and the adult" (Vygotsky 1978, p. 169).

Vygotsky's views on affect

Despite the recent lack of attention afforded to the role of affect and personal relationships, it is clear that Vygotsky himself understood their centrality in cognitive development. For example, his oft-quoted definition of the learning process cited earlier in this article concludes with the sentence: "All the higher functions originate as actual relations between human individuals" (Vygotsky 1978, p. 57). In *Thought and Language* (Vygotsky, 1962, p. 8), Vygotsky resisted the separation of cognition and affect, emphasizing instead "the existence of a dynamic system of meaning in which the affective and the intellectual unite." Similarly, Vygotsky's 1931 assertion that "the adolescent's emotional and intellectual aspects of behavior achieve their synthesis in his creative imagination" (Vygotsky, cited in van der Veer and Valsiner, 1994, p. 286) suggests that he viewed cognition and affect as integrated and interdependent.

Unfortunately, however, Vygotsky did little empirical research into the affective aspects of consciousness, and direct discussion of affect emerges infrequently in his writings (Wertsch, 1985). Had

Vygotsky not met an untimely death from tuberculosis at the age of 37, it is likely that he would have turned his formidable intellect to the role of affect in learning relationships. Indeed, Vygotsky's student L.I. Bozhovich asserts Vygotsky "devoted the entire last period of his life to a theoretical development of the problem of affect, its relationship to intellectual processes," but indicates this "next stage in the development of Vygotsky's scientific thought ...was never completed and expressed in print" (Bozhovich, 1977, p. 15).[3]

Because the depth and breadth of Vygotsky's thinking on the role played by affect in teaching-learning relationships was never fully documented, we are left with the challenge of piecing together Vygotsky's understanding of this phenomenon by combing through his collected writings. One of the problems endemic to work on Vygotsky is that, for many scholars, it is only possible to read his works in translation. This puts us in the hands of the translators and the editors: each translator and each editor makes decisions about what to include, what to omit, and how best to communicate the intent and the content of Vygotsky's original text. As a result, reading two different translations of the same text can unearth previously unconsidered perspectives and can lead to very different conclusions.

Vygotsky's article "Tool and symbol in child development," comprises the first four chapters of *Mind and Society* (Vygotsky, 1978), edited by Michael Cole, Vera John-Steiner, Sylvia Scribner & Ellen Souberman. According to these editors, a rough English translation of this 1930 article was presented to them by Vygotsky's colleague Alexander Luria, and, after additional translation by Michael Cole, the text was edited and prepared for

---

[3]Bozhovich herself has explored some of this terrain, drawing on Vygotsky's work to develop a model of human development integrating the cognitive and the affective. For example, she writes: "The formation of the personality should proceed in such a way that the cognitive and affective processes, and hence both what is controllable and what is not controllable by the conscious mind, are brought into a certain harmonious relationship with one another" (Bozhovich, 1979, p. 7).

publication. In reflecting on their editing process, they write: "We have taken significant liberties. The reader will encounter here not a literal translation of Vygotsky but rather our edited translation of Vygotsky from which we have omitted material that seemed redundant and to which we have added material that seemed to make his points clearer" (Cole, John-Steiner, Scribner & Souberman 1978, p. x). While this is a common practice, it seemed possible that material they might have found redundant would be useful in highlighting Vygotsky's views on the role of affect in the ZPD.

The recently published volume *The Vygotsky Reader*, edited by Rene van der Veer & Jaan Valsiner (1994), offers readers a somewhat different version of "Tool and symbol in child development." Van der Veer & Valsiner began with the same text as the editors of *Mind and Society*, but rather than editing, adding, and omitting, they elected to compare the English translation which Luria provided to Cole to the original Russian text of 1930, and then attempted to present their text in a version as faithful to the original as possible. In this version, Vygotsky (and Luria, who received credit as co-author in this version, just as he did in the Russian version noted by Vygotsky in his 1934 bibliography) discusses affect several times; these particular passages are not included in the text of the article presented in *Mind and Society*.

For example, Vygotsky and Luria (in van der Veer & Valsiner, 1994, p. 115) write:

> Our records show that from the very earliest stages of the child's development, the factor moving his activities from one level to another is neither repetition nor discovery. The source of development of these activities is to be found in the social environment of the child and is manifest in concrete form in those specific relations with the experimentalist which transcend the entire situation requiring the practical use of tools and introduce into it a social aspect. In order to express in one formula the essence of those forms of infant behavior, characteristic of the earliest stage of development, it must be noted that the child enters into relations with the situation not directly, but through the medium of another person.

In stating "the source of development of these activities is to be found in the social environment of the child and is manifest in concrete form in those specific relations with the experimentalist which transcend the entire situation," Vygotsky and Luria make clear the fundamental importance of one-on-one interpersonal relationships to learning and development: the zone of proximal development is also a relational zone.

That relationships are the main route to intellectual development is apparent in another quote from the same text (Vygotsky & Luria, in van der Veer & Valsiner, 1994, p. 116):

> The entire history of the child's psychological development shows us that, from the very first days of development, its adaptation to the environment is achieved by social means, through the people surrounding him. The road from object to child and from child to object lies through another person. . . . This road—passing through another person—proves to be the central highway of development of practical intellect.

Vygotsky has often been criticized for ignoring affective issues (Newman & Holzman, 1993, Rogoff, 1990). Dean (1994, p. 5), for example, expresses concern that absent from Vygotsky's work "is the living, feeling person who experiences changes in his or her relationship to the object world and who acts according to these subjective experiences." This is not the case. In fact, Vygotsky & Luria wrote just the opposite: in describing a particular experiment, they state "the child views the situation as a problem posed by the experimentalist, and he senses that, present or not, a human being stands behind the problem" (Vygotsky & Luria, in van der Veer & Valsiner, 1994, p. 116). The human element is certainly present in Vygotsky's own writings. Though it may have been overlooked in many of the summaries and interpretations of his work, Vygotsky himself saw affect and intellect as interconnected and inseparable.

Exploring the relational zone

Scholars building on Vygotsky emphasize the central importance of context in cognitive growth; interpersonal relationships
are simply an assumed, implicit contour of the contextual terrain.
I contend that relationships must be considered explicitly in these
discussions of context, beyond the ways described by Moll &
Whitmore (1993), Palincsar et al. (1993), Rogoff et al. (1984), Tharp
(1993), and Wood et al. (1978): the affective qualities of the
relationship between teacher and student—what I have labeled
the interrelational dimension—are what allows the zone of
proximal development to take shape in any given situation.

Allusions to the role and the value of affect and interpersonal
relationships in cognitive development can be found in the work
of scholars who draw upon Vygotsky's theories. However, they
are rarely considered in depth. Barbara Rogoff, for example,
writes "there is more to intersubjectivity than just thinking—
thinking, feeling, and emotion are all part of it" (Rogoff, 1990, p.
9). In their Vygotsky-centered book on scaffolding children's
development, Berk & Winsler (1994, p. 29) begin a sub-section
with the heading "Warmth and responsiveness," and state:
"Another important component of scaffolding concerns the
emotional tone of the interaction. Children's engagement with a
task and willingness to challenge themselves are maximized when
collaboration with the adult is pleasant, warm, and responsive."

Stone (1993, p. 170) notes that "the effectiveness of interactions
(and therefore the potential for new learning) within the ZPD
varies as a function of the interpersonal relationship between the
participants," and brings in Rommetveit's (1974) commentary on
the importance of "mutual trust" in the process of intersubjectivity. Further, Stone points out that the nature of a dyad's
intersubjective exchanges "is a function of the past, present, and
anticipated future interactions between the participants" (Stone,
1993, p. 178), and indicates that an individual's learning opportunities in the zone of proximal development must be understood

as situated in a "complex interpersonal context" (Stone, 1993, p. 179).

Also aware of the complex interpersonal context of the zone of proximal development, Goodnow (1993, p. 376) asks an interesting question: "Could a mother who demonstrated effective methods with her own child use them also with another child?" Implicit here is a query about the degree to which the nature of the particular relationship between the individuals collaborating within the ZPD impacts the power and efficacy of the strategies used. Goodnow's question could be re-worded to ask: "In what way does the specific relationship between the child and the adult affect the learning potential of the dyad?"

Generally, when relational issues arise in the empirical literature, they are dealt with only obliquely. For example, Wood, Bruner & Ross (1976, pp. 92-3) make one brief but intriguing allusion to the affective dimension of the zone of proximal development. In describing their study, in which a tutor scaffolded children as they solved a wooden puzzle, they indicate that the personality and affect of the tutor impacted the outcome of the study. They write:

> The tutor . . . brought to the task a gentle, appreciative approach to the children. She did not so much praise them directly for their constructions or for their attention to the task, but rather created such an atmosphere of approval that the children seemed eager to complete their constructions—often, seemingly, to show her as well as to reach the goal per se. A testing procedure and a tutor create an atmosphere of encouragement or discouragement: in the present case it was the former, *and the results certainly reflect it.* [emphasis mine]

In this statement, Wood, Bruner & Ross acknowledge the power of a caring stance in affecting children's learning and achievement.

In her work on peer interactions in mathematical problem solving, Forman (1989) also makes an implicit reference to the power of relationship to effect children's learning and achievement. She found the evolving nature of the relationship between a pair of girls working together on a problem-solving task corresponded to the degree of progress made by the pair. In designing this study, Forman deliberately selected subjects who "declared themselves to be best friends" (Forman, 1989, p. 60). Obviously, this fact would make a difference in the success or failure of the collaborating dyad. Had Forman randomly chosen girls who did not like each other, she would have had different results: the girls' working relationship would have been adversely affected by the nature and quality of their personal relationship. In carefully choosing subjects based on the strength of the interpersonal relationship they brought to the task initially, Forman tacitly acknowledges the power of certain kinds of relationships in intersubjectivity, in the zone of proximal development, and, therefore, in cognitive development and intellectual growth.

Nel Noddings and the ethic of care

The literature suggests that interpersonal relationship can be considered a significant factor in cognitive development. I believe our understanding of this interrelational dimension of the zone of proximal development can be enhanced through the application of feminist moral theory, specifically the ethic of care. The ethic of care, developed "to deal with the regions of experience that have been central to women's experience and neglected by traditional moral theory" (Held, 1987, p. 114), is centered around interpersonal connection. Vygotsky believed strongly in the value of human relationships in learning and development, however he did not articulate these ideas fully. The ethic of care, specifically the work of Nel Noddings that I described in detail in chapter 1, provides an explication of the nature and the role of teaching-learning relationships, thereby picking up where Vygotsky left off.

Noddings asserts that caring is an essential quality of meaningful teaching. She writes: "the teacher is necessarily one-caring if she is to be a teacher and not simply a textbooklike source from which the student may or may not learn" (Noddings,

1984, p. 70). A caring teacher's practices are informed both by an understanding of what must be done, and by a sense of what ought to be done.

Noddings describes the manner in which a teacher acting as one-caring would go about her work. As in any caring encounter, receptivity and engrossment are the first steps. She says: "If I care about students [who are attempting to solve a problem], I must do two things: I must make the problem my own, receive it intellectually, immerse myself in it; I must also bring the students into proximity, receive such students personally" (Noddings, 1984, p.113).

This is followed by motivational displacement: after the teacher receives a student and feels with him, she looks at the problem "through his eyes and ears . . . . She accepts *his* motives, reaches toward what *he* intends" (Noddings, 1984, p. 177). The caring encounter is completed when the student responds to the teacher's caring, rewarding her "with questions, effort, comment, and cooperation" (Noddings, 1984, p. 181).

It is possible, then, for adults to remain in the role of one-caring for extended periods of time when interacting with children, provided the children's responses suggest some pleasant form of acknowledgment. The cared-for's reciprocity need not be a formal expression of gratitude; expecting such from young children, for example, might be inappropriate. A student who responds to his teacher simply by wordlessly nodding his head and hurrying back to his desk to return to work has offered a response as rewarding to a teacher as an explicit "thank you" would be.

Using a metaphor frequently used in discussions of Vygotsky and socially mediated cognition (Lave & Wenger, 1991, Rogoff, 1990) in her discussion of caring teaching-learning relationships, Noddings evokes the image of the student as an apprentice. She writes: "The teacher works with the student. He becomes her apprentice and gradually assumes greater responsibility in the tasks they undertake. This working together . . . produces joy in the relation and increasing competence in the cared-for"

(Noddings, 1984, p.177-8). In referring to the joy inherent in the teaching-learning relation, Noddings reveals the affective dimension of the apprenticeship model that has been invisible in other accounts of the metaphor.

By focusing on these relational issues, Noddings captures and conveys what others have overlooked: the joyful quality of teaching, and the pleasures of being intimately involved with a child's growth and learning. In discussing the character of the caring teaching-learning relationship, Noddings reminds us that "there is mutual pleasure not only in the child's growing competence, but also in the shared activities and their products" (Noddings, 1984, p. 63). The strength of the particular picture Noddings has painted here lies in its reciprocal nature: both the teacher and the student are deriving pleasure from the learning, from the activities, from the fruits of their shared labor, and from their relationship with each other.

When Noddings writes about the nature of the caring teacher-student relationship, the language she uses parallels descriptions of the experience of a teacher and a student working together in the student's zone of proximal development. For example, Noddings states that the teacher has two major responsibilities: "to stretch the student's world by presenting an effective selection of that world with which she is in contact, and to work cooperatively with the student in his struggle toward competence in that world" (Noddings, 1984, p. 178). Further, Noddings's belief that "the teacher must see things through the eyes of her student in order to teach him" (Noddings, 1984, p. 70), and her assertion that a teacher must base her educational decisions depending not on rules "but upon a constellation of conditions that is viewed through both the eyes of the one-caring and the eyes of the cared-for" (Noddings, 1984, p. 13) sound remarkably like some of the descriptions of intersubjectivity written by Vygotsky-informed scholars.

Laying Noddings's terminology for caring encounters over existing descriptions of intersubjectivity reveals the affective, relational dimensions of the process and the experience. My intent is not to suggest that Noddings's work and Vygotsky's work match up in perfect alignment but to use Noddings's understanding of caring, and the vocabulary which emerges from it, to highlight the interrelational dimensions of the zone of proximal development, dimensions which Vygotsky alluded to but never detailed.

In their discussion of intersubjectivity, for example, Rogoff and Wertsch point out that the adult and the child "do not have the same definition of the task or of the problem to be solved" (1984, p. 5), and indicate it is imperative that the adult makes an effort to comprehend the child's understanding of the task at hand. To use Noddings's phraseology to describe this intersubjective phenomenon, the adult must begin the caring learning encounter with engrossment and receptivity: she must fully receive the child, seeing the problem as if through that child's eyes.

An adult working with a child in the zone of proximal development must be prepared to act in a non-rulebound manner on behalf of the child. Each child brings a particular set of skills and interests to bear on any given problem. The adult has particular responsibility for segmenting the task into subgoals manageable for that specific child, and for altering the child's definition of the task to make it increasingly compatible with expert performance (Rogoff & Wertsch, 1984, p. 5). In Noddings's description of a caring encounter, she also mentions this phenomenon, writing that the teacher, as one-caring, "watches for incipient interest in the child — the particular, concrete child — and arranges the educational environment accordingly" (Noddings, 1984, p. 63). The caring adult must respond to the child in a way that emphasizes "the uniqueness of human encounters" (Noddings, 1984, p. 5), acting not by some "fixed rule, but by affection and regard" (Noddings, 1984, p. 24).

By speaking of this well-discussed aspect of scaffolding using the vocabulary of affection and regard, Noddings brings to the fore the affective dimension of the zone of proximal development.

In another example of this, Noddings describes a typical teaching-learning encounter using the language of care:

> When a teacher asks a question in class and a student responds, she receives not just the "response" but the student. What he says matters, whether it is right or wrong, and she probes gently for clarification, interpretation, contribution. She is not seeking the answer but the involvement of the cared-for. (Noddings, 1984, p. 176)

In pointing out that the teacher receives not only the response but also the student, and in indicating that the teacher is committed more to drawing the student into the learning process than to arriving at the correct answer, Noddings's description highlights relational features of the zone of proximal development which have previously been in the shadows. In addition to meshing well with our existing understanding of intersubjectivity and the zone of proximal development, Noddings's descriptions enrich our thinking about these teaching-learning relationships by making clear the deep feelings that accompany those interactions, adding an affective dimension—joy, pleasure, satisfaction, connection, caring—to our definition.

Growth and transformation in the ZPD

Merging Noddings's work on caring with the existing body of literature on the zone of proximal development suggests that entering the zone creates a range of opportunities for intellectual growth and personal transformation. These developments occur both on the interpsychological level and the interrelational level, for both the adult and the child. The roles played by the adult and the child—as teacher and student and as one-caring and cared-for—in teaching-learning interactions in the ZPD expose each to different opportunities for change, and different types of change, at different points in the encounter.

Addressing the interpsychological dimension first, discussions of intersubjectivity in the zone of proximal development indicate both the adult and the child must change as they negotiate shared meaning. Both partners adapt to each other, "with their mutual adjustments facilitating interpersonal understanding for the purpose of communication and changing the nature of the understanding that they may bring to other situations" (Rogoff, 1990, p. 73). Further, the intersubjective understanding itself is not static, but grows and transforms itself over the duration of the learning encounter. The student learns and moves up through his ZPD, altering his understanding of the task. Simultaneously, the teacher should take note of the strategies the student found most useful, thus enriching her understanding of the student and enhancing her ability to provide appropriate support specifically tailored to his needs. Inter-psychological meaning is negotiated and re-negotiated throughout the learning encounter.

Though both emerge changed, the teacher and the student experience different types of intellectual transformation during a teaching-learning encounter. The student experiences lasting changes in cognition. As Rogoff points out: "Less able to adjust to ensure communication, but more in need of developing under-standing (and more willing to change), children stretch to understand the interpretations available in interaction with their caregivers and companions" (Rogoff, 1990, p. 74). Because adults enter the interaction with a more sophisticated understanding of the problem, the only changes they are required to make are those temporary adjustments that facilitate their interaction with the child: these changes "by no means indicate a shift in his opinion of how the objects and events in the task setting are most appropriately understood or represented" (Wertsch, 1984, p. 13).

Though teachers do not need to stretch their cognitive faculties in the same way that their students must during teaching-learning interactions, teachers do not emerge from these encounters unchanged: teaching-learning interactions with students are teachers' central loci of professional growth and development. Interacting with students in their zones of proximal development transforms novice teachers into seasoned professionals (Berliner,

1986). For example, in reflecting on their professional training, teachers have long asserted that they learned to teach through field experience rather than formal coursework (Lortie, 1975). Grossman and Richert (1988, p. 59) insist that "the fieldwork experience provokes this growth of knowledge by allowing opportunities for teacher-student interactions."

Along similar lines, when Wilson & Wineburg (1993, p. 742) describe a teacher as approaching a task "with the confidence of someone who has spent 27 years grading papers;" when Shulman (1986) refers to his notion of "pedagogical content knowledge; " and when Cochran-Smith & Lytle (1990) assert that classroom teachers should be primary contributors to our knowledge base about teaching, all are acknowledging the central importance of "the wisdom of practice" (Shulman, 1986, p. 9) – garnered as a result of many teaching-learning encounters with many students – in teachers' professional capabilities.

The literature on the interpsychological dimension of the zone of proximal development indicates that the adult and the child adapt and adjust their thinking while working together in the ZPD and are both permanently transformed, though in different ways, as a result of the interaction. Using Noddings's work as a blueprint suggests that the interrelational level functions in a slightly different manner.

In contrast to the interpsychological dimension, only the adult – the one-caring – adapts and adjusts during a teaching-learning encounter. To illustrate this point, Noddings draws upon her experience as a mathematics teacher dealing with a student who claims to hate math. She wonders how it would feel to hate mathematics: "I begin, as nearly as I can, with the view from his eyes: Mathematics is bleak, jumbled, scary, boring, boring, boring . . . . What in the world could induce me to engage in it? From that point on we struggle together with it" (Noddings, 1984, p. 15-6). The one-caring receives the cared-for, and attempts to replace her own understanding of the situation with his, and his motives become hers for the duration of the caring encounter. The cared-for, on the other hand, does not receive the one-caring. He does not need to change at all during the course of the caring encounter; the cared-for simply needs to acknowledge the care he has received.

However, as with the interpsychological dimension, both the adult and child are transformed on the interrelational level as a result of their teaching-learning encounter. The one-caring enhances her ethical ideal and the cared-for emerges stronger for having entered into a caring relation. Noddings (1984, p. 20) states:

> the cared-for glows, grows stronger, and feels not so much that he has been given something as that something has been added to him. And this "something" may be hard to specify. Indeed, for the one-caring and the cared-for in a relationship of genuine caring, there is no felt need on either part to specify what sort of transformation has taken place.

Broadening our discussion of the zone of proximal development to include both its intellectual and its affective and volitional dimensions makes clear the many ways that both adult and child contribute to and are changed by the experience of connecting in the ZPD. In addition to being a region of intellectual development—a construction zone—the zone of proximal development is also a region of affective development—a relational zone.

Motivation and volition

Given the interpersonal effort involved, and the inevitability of change accompanying engagement in teaching-learning encounters of this kind, why would adults and children elect to work together in creating zones of proximal development? Vygotsky recognized, but did not address, the question of motivation and volition (Bozhovich, 1977; Litowitz, 1993). The contemporary literature on the zone of proximal development has likewise overlooked this issue (Litowitz, 1993), operating on the implicit assumption that adults and children involved in these teaching-learning encounters are always eager, benevolent, responsive, and enthusiastic.

Litowitz notes that in most of the literature on teaching-learning interactions the zone of proximal development features flawlessly functioning dyads moving through the "official" stages smoothly and with few obstacles: "The positive intent of both participants is rarely questioned; similarly, the smooth efficiency is rarely doubted" (Litowitz, 1993, p. 187). Goodnow (1990, p. 279) also notes these shortcomings in the literature on the zone of proximal development:

> My disappointment with the picture usually presented is that once again the world is benign and relatively neutral. To be more specific, the standard picture is one of willing teachers on the one hand and eager learners on the other. Where are the parents who do not see their role as one of imparting information and encouraging understanding? Where are the children who do not wish to learn or perform in the first place, or who regard as useless what the teaching adult is presenting?

Drawing on Kaye (1982) in her attempt to address the motivation question, Litowitz (1993) suggests humans may have some sort of innate pedagogical drive. Kaye (1982) points out that most animals demonstrate the skills necessary for survival; their offspring learn by watching. By contrast, humans—mothers, fathers, siblings and peers, acquaintances and community members—teach their young directly. Kaye asserts that this process developed over time in response to the challenging task of becoming human.

Noddings's work offers different answers to the motivation question. She writes:

> We are *obligated* to do what is required to maintain and enhance caring. We must "justify" not-caring; that is, we must explain why, in the interest of caring for ourselves as ethical selves or in the interest of others for whom we care, we may behave as ones-not-caring" (Noddings, 1984, p. 95, italics in original).

Adults enter into relationships of this nature, including teaching-learning encounters, because it is a moral imperative.

Children, on the other hand, will often engage in the challenges offered by adult ones-caring "if the one-caring is loved and trusted by the child. As an initial impulse to engage particular subject matter, love for the adult and the desire to imitate her are powerful inducements" (Noddings, 1984, p. 64). Noddings's assertion echoes Wood, Bruner & Ross's observation that the children in their study "seemed eager to complete their constructions—often, seemingly, to show [the tutor] as well as to reach the goal per se" (Wood, Bruner & Ross, 1976, pp. 92-3). These children were simply participants in a brief research study, yet because of the tutor's "gentle, appreciative approach to the children" and her ability to create "an atmosphere of approval" (Wood, Bruner & Ross, 1976, pp. 92-3), they were fully willing to enter into a teaching-learning relationship with her and were eager to meet with her approval.

Along similar lines, in my study of the role of loving relationships in Martha George's teaching practices discussed in chapter 1, I marveled at the children's willingness to accept me fully as a teacher in their classroom, eagerly completing their work and showing it to me proudly. I asked Martha, "What reason could they possibly have to invest their emotions in me?" Martha, the teacher, responded, "Does it have to do with youth and innocence? Perhaps children only need reasons NOT to love or care for people, and are otherwise willing to open themselves and their hearts" (Goldstein, 1997, p. 86).

Looking at the zone of proximal development as a locus of connection and relationship offers a new perspective on the intriguing question of motivation. An interaction in the ZPD is both intellectually rewarding and emotionally satisfying for the adult and the child involved. Adults and children are motivated to enter into teaching-learning encounters by the pleasure, the growth, and the interpersonal connection they provide. The zone of proximal development is a space to experience the particular joys of being human. This is the pedagogical power of caring.

The major implication of this enhanced view of the knowledge-making process is the conclusion that caring relationships are a central part of intellectual growth and development. Others have suggested that teacherly caring raises children's self esteem and sense of belonging in the classroom (Charney, 1991; Dalton & Watson, 1997), and creates an atmosphere of trust that enables children to take risks (McDermott, 1977); I believe this to be true. However, if the research indicating that children learn through socially mediated encounters is correct, then caring relationships, as a necessary and fundamental part of an intersubjective encounter, actually enable and lead to cognitive development.

This is a conclusion of profound importance. Caring must be reclaimed and made central in our educational environments because of its crucial role in intellectual growth. Developing teacher education programs centered around caring is one strategy to reach that goal. It is crucial, however, that the moral and intellectual relation view of caring be the operational definition of caring at the heart of such teacher education programs. Because of its rootedness in relation, only the moral and intellectual relation view of caring provides a means to tap into the pedagogical power of caring.

The moral and intellectual relation view of caring is also tremendously important for teachers because it offers a foundation for a professional stance that captures the complexity, the artistry, the challenge, and the significance of the work we do with children, and provides a sound foundation for teacher education for reasons in addition to those linked to the pedagogical power of caring. In the following chapters, I describe a recent study I undertook as the first steps toward the development of an approach to teacher education rooted in the moral and intellectual relation view of caring.

SECTION II

LEARNING ABOUT CARING TEACHING: PRESERVICE TEACHERS' PERSPECTIVES AND REFLECTIONS

Chapter 3

Preservice Teachers and Caring

Caring is considered a crucial aspect of good teaching from early childhood education (Bredekamp & Copple, 1997) to the teaching of adults (Arnstine, 1990; Courtney, 1992; Estes, 1994; Rogers & Webb, 1991; Rosiek, 1994), and across virtually all academic disciplines (Alter, 1995; Damarin, 1994; Lamme & McKinley, 1992; Rasinski, 1990; Robicheaux, 1996; Rust, 1994; Sickle & Spector, 1996). As I have argued, caring is a powerful professional stance for teachers. And, most importantly, the moral and intellectual relation view of caring creates teaching-learning opportunities necessary for intellectual growth and development. In order to reclaim caring, putting the moral and intellectual relation view of caring at the center of our educational endeavors where it belongs, it is necessary to begin with teacher education.

As teacher educators, we must strive to create curricula and preparation programs that engender in preservice teachers an understanding of the power of caring as a moral and intellectual relation and a commitment to implementing care-centered teaching practices in their classrooms (Goodlad, Soder & Sirotnik, 1990; Noddings, 1986). As Arnstine said, "If teacher educators want to further the aims of caring . . . in schooling, then the means must be the cultivation of appropriate activities in the teacher education program" (Arnstine, 1990, p. 244).

This process of program development could have many starting points. A review of the scholarly literature on caring in teacher education revealed that surprisingly little work has been done in this area. Scholars such as Noddings (1986) and Rogers & Webb (1991) have offered theoretical models for reconceptualizing and reshaping teacher education. A small handful of others have made suggestions about ways in which our existing teacher education programs could be strengthened through the ethic of care. Rosiek (1994), for example, suggests the use of

narrative case studies; Swick (1999) offers service learning;
Arnstine (1990) advocates the creation of collaborative learning
communities and emphasizes the importance of developing relevant curricula linking theory to problems emerging in the preservice teachers' classroom practice contexts.

In a related study, Thayer-Bacon, Arnold & Stoots (1998)
gathered information from preservice teachers at their university
in an effort to identify which of the teacher education professors
were considered most caring. Thayer-Bacon et al. believe, as I do,
that caring teaching-learning relationships help students learn;
they saw their study as a first step toward developing recommen-
dations about how teacher education professors could build on
the pedagogical power of caring in their work with preservice
teachers. Thayer-Bacon et al. captured the underlying message of
all of the studies summarized here when they said that the value
of caring teaching "is especially important for professors in
teacher education programs to understand, as we are the
professors who are modeling good teaching to the next generation
of teachers" (Thayer-Bacon et al., 1998, p. 5).

Like Noddings, Rogers & Webb, Thayer-Bacon et al. and the
others scholars cited above, I am eager to improve teacher
education through the ethic of caring. However, before making
any suggestions about the best ways to enhance our ability to
educate preservice teachers about the value of caring, I felt it was
essential to get insight into some fundamental issues first. I
wanted to develop a clear sense both of the working
understandings of caring brought by preservice teachers to their
teacher education experiences (Bullough, 1991; Hollingsworth,
1989) and of the ways that those beliefs are challenged, affirmed,
or transformed during their student teaching period. In this
chapter, I describe the study I designed in order to learn more
about preservice teachers' beliefs about and experiences with
caring teaching.

Study procedures

In the spring of 1998, assisted by Vickie Lake, who served as teaching assistant and field placement supervisor, I conducted a two-part study of preservice teachers' understandings of caring.[1] Participants were members of a cohort of preservice teachers — seventeen undergraduates and two post-baccalaureate students — enrolled in my Elementary Classroom Organization and Management course at a large research university in the southern United States.

This Classroom Organization and Management course is a central requirement for our teacher education students' professional development sequence, and provides the cohort students with their first long-term field placement. In this placement, students spend 20 hours per week in an elementary classroom (grades 1-5) in a socio-culturally diverse urban school district for a period of 10 weeks.[2] Half of the students in our cohort were placed in high poverty, high minority schools and half were in middle class, primarily white schools; in their second field placement in the subsequent semester, the preservice teachers switched student populations to experience both types of school contexts.

The Classroom Organization and Management course met weekly, and covered topics such as classroom environments, discipline, lesson and unit planning, professionalism, and so on. In addition to the goals of preparing students for the challenges of organizing and managing an elementary classroom and supporting students during their first extended field placement, this particular course also exists to prepare our students to pass the statewide licensure examination. Although the general content and topics of the course are predetermined by the content of the exam, course instructors have a fair amount of leeway for creativity and individualization of the syllabus and of instruction within that framework.

---

[1]Vickie Lake also participated in data analysis for this study.

[2]In the following semester, the students engage in their formal student teaching work.

During the semester that this study was underway, my focus on and commitment to the development of caring teachers and the creation of caring classrooms was made clear to the students through my choice of materials, assignments, and activities; through my attempts to model caring teaching practices and to discuss those practices explicitly; and through the students' knowledge about and participation in the caring study. I was explicit about the distinctions between the gentle smiles and warm hugs view and the moral and intellectual relation view of caring, and Noddings's work was read and discussed in detail in class.

In order to facilitate and support reflection, electronic dialogue journals were an integral part of the structure of this course (McIntyre & Tlusty, 1995); in addition to being a course requirement, these dialogue journals also provided the data set for this study. Each student in the class reflected and wrote weekly journal entries on topics related to the role of caring in their placement classroom experiences and emailed their thoughts to me. I responded to each student's reflective writing individually in ways that I hoped would encourage the student to explore and respond to the theme of caring in classrooms in a way that furthered his or her individual growth as a professional and deepened his or her thinking on the role of relationships in teaching.

These weekly writings, exchanged between me and each student via electronic mail, were nicknamed "ejournals." I opted for electronic dialogue journals for several reasons. First, the preservice teacher education students at our university are expected to develop their technological literacy; every course is expected to have some technology component.[3] Second, I believed that the email format would provide students with a less formal, more spontaneous medium than traditional notebook-style journals

---

[3]In addition to the ejournals, we also used email as a regular form of communication within the class. Further, we created a class listserve that allowed all members of the cohort—students, supervisor, course instructors, and faculty coordinators—to communicate easily with the group as a whole.

(Tella, 1992), thereby eliminating some of the pressure and drudgery often associated with reflective journal writing (Maas, 1991). Email journals also allowed me to respond quickly to the students' writings; the ejournals became a way for students to get feedback on pressing classroom issues in a timely manner.

Participation in this study of caring was open to all students in the class; data comprised the weekly dialogue journal responses assigned as a course requirement. All students in the cohort wrote these ejournal responses; only those students who elected to participate in the study—sixteen female and one male, with a range of ethnicities including Anglo, Asian, and Hispanic—had their responses considered as data for this project.[4]

The data were independently read and coded by myself and by Vickie. Data were analyzed horizontally, by looking at each individual student's writing across the semester; and vertically, by looking at the week-by-week gestalt of the cohort as a whole. Themes which emerged in both my and Vickie's analyses were highlighted, explored in greater depth, and interpreted. The key themes running through the data relating to the student teachers' preconceptions or initial understandings about the relationships between teaching and caring were extracted and considered as Phase 1 of the study. The themes emerging from the students' experiences enacting caring teaching in their field placement classrooms were considered as Phase 2 of the study.

---

[4]Students were assured that their decision to participate or to abstain from participation in this study would not affect their workload for the course, their grade, our evaluation of their work, or their future relationships with the university. Study participants were aware that, in addition to being read by me, their instructor, in the context of the course, their journal entries would be analyzed, interpreted, and, in all likelihood, made public as part of the study; all participants gave their full permission. Of the 19 students enrolled in the cohort, 17 chose to participate in the study.

Phase 1: Initial understandings of caring

In the first part of the study, I explored the preservice teachers' preconceptions and initial beliefs about caring and about the relationship between caring and teaching. Although caring is a term whose meaning is often unclear and misunderstood in relation to actual teaching practices (Rogers & Webb, 1991), preservice teachers nevertheless enter their professional preparation programs with tacit definitions of caring and with a range of ideas and beliefs about the ways that caring will play out in their teaching lives.

These ideas and beliefs about caring have developed over the course of the students' experiences in a variety of teaching-learning situations over a period of many years. These ideas have been shaped by pervasive cultural scripts which link women, caring, and the career of elementary schoolteaching (Acker, 1999; Biklen, 1995; Burgess & Carter, 1992; Grumet, 1988). These connections are very strong and have deep roots in Western history. At the heart of this linkage is an unspoken, assumed association of women and mothering. The act of women caring for young children has been positioned as "natural." And so, by extension, the occupation of women teaching young children also appears natural. Women, children, caring, and teaching are inextricably intertwined in our culture in the United States and in many other Western nations.

These cultural scripts, assumptions, and associations are reinforced by reality. While it has been argued that the child-centered pedagogy that characterizes elementary schooling is rooted in ideas of care and nurturance that are associated with women in potentially problematic ways (Grumet, 1988; Walkerdine, 1986), it is also true that most elementary school teachers are women. During our preservice teachers' lengthy apprenticeships of observation (Lortie, 1975), it is likely that they watched these pedagogical practices enacted by women teachers many times over. The marriage of caring, teaching and the female sex played out in our students' childhood classrooms and shaped their thinking about their future profession.

These images of caring female teachers are further reinscribed for our students throughout their childhoods by so many of the fictitious representations of teachers we see on television and in the movies, in children's literature and in the comics (Joseph & Burnaford, 1994). As our students grow up, they see these same images re-presented and embodied by the real teachers celebrated as heroes on television talk shows and in the popular press. Students drawn to teacher narratives and teacher novels (Isenberg, 1994) such as *Up the Down Staircase* (Kaufman, 1964), Sylvia Ashton-Warner's *Teacher* (Ashton-Warner, 1963), as many of our preservice teachers are, are further exposed to these stereotypical images of caring female teachers.

A large body of research on teacher beliefs indicates that biography, previous experiences, and preconceived ideas will be a strong influence on the student teachers' understandings of and experiences in their classroom placements (Cole & Knowles, 1993; Lortie, 1975; Silvernail & Costello, 1983; Tabachnick & Zeichner, 1984; Zeichner & Grant, 1991; Zeichner & Tabachnick, 1981). Kagan (1992) reviewed 27 qualitative studies published between 1987 and 1991 that documented the experiences of preservice teachers. She concluded: "Each study documented the central role played by preexisting beliefs/images and prior experience in filtering the content of education course work" (Kagan, 1992, p. 140).

Bullough (1991) offers a constructivist explanation for this phenomenon. He points out that preservice teachers enter their teacher education programs with a great deal of prior knowledge about teaching; this prior knowledge "serves as a filter through which the student responds to teacher education" (Bullough, 1991, p. 43). New information that makes sense in relation to this pre-existing knowledge base is accepted and that which does not is rejected.

Cole & Knowles (1993) also acknowledge the influence of preservice teachers' prior knowledge. But they warn that preservice teachers' preconceptions about teaching are formed based on limited experience with and understanding of the realities of teaching, and as a result are likely to be inadequate, partial, and disconnected from the particularities of actual classroom practices. Because of this, it has been argued that teacher educators "should come to understand the incoming beliefs of [their] students" (Hollingsworth, 1989, p. 161), attend carefully to those beliefs, and endeavor to build on them in productive ways within teacher education programs (Bullough, 1991; Dunkin, Precians & Nettle, 1994) . Thus, I attempted to learn more about my preservice teachers' incoming beliefs about caring and teaching.

I was concerned that the inarticulated and unexamined understandings of caring brought by preservice teachers to their first professional experiences would mold these novice teachers' practices and shape their emerging images of themselves as educators. Because of the strong influence of prior knowledge and the sense that preservice teachers' preconceived understandings are likely to be strongly-held and fairly stable (Kagan, 1992), I suspected that I would be facing a group of "gentle smilers and warm huggers." My goal in Phase I of this study was to get a baseline reading on the students' understandings and use this new knowledge as a starting point for educative dialogue and interactions that would deepen and enrich the students' understandings of caring. My hope for Phase II was to see the ways that these gentle smilers and warm huggers matured into the type of caring teachers I envisioned—moral and intellectual relaters able to capitalize on the pedagogical power of caring.

Phase 2: Belief changes during the field placement period

The study's second goal was to explore the ways in which my preservice teachers' understandings of caring were affected by their field placement experiences. The literature on preservice teacher socialization suggests that placement in the field can be challenging and destabilizing for students: preconceptions and aspirations collide with reality (Cole & Knowles, 1993). When this occurs, ideas and beliefs previously embraced during teacher education coursework are often cast aside (Zeichner & Tabach-nick, 1981).

During the field placement experience students are subjected to influence from cooperating teachers and from other classroom-based and institutional factors (Zeichner & Grant, 1991) that can lead to increasingly conservative and traditional beliefs (Zeichner, 1980) or to more bureaucratic and impersonal practices (Hoy & Rees, 1977). Hoy & Woolfolk (1990) found, for example, that preservice teachers became more custodial and controlling toward their students as a result of their student teaching experiences. Their message is disheartening: they write, "the ideal images of college preparation apparently give way to the instrumental necessities of maintaining order and running a smoothly function-ing classroom" (Hoy & Woolfolk, 1990, p. 294).

Similarly, Zeichner (1980) describes some preservice teachers abandoning thoughtful and reflective teaching practice and adopt-ing a more utilitarian approach: "as students spend time in the field, getting the class through the required lesson on time in a quiet and orderly manner becomes the major criterion for accept-ing or rejecting a teaching activity" (Zeichner, 1980, p. 49).

During their field placement period, then, student teachers' images of themselves as teachers and their understandings of the contours of the job of teaching are in a state of flux. Although certain preconceptions are robust and fairly stable (Kagan, 1992), the challenges of fieldwork can call certain assumptions into ques-tion. Further, it appears that attitudes and understandings learned during university coursework are easily forgotten and replaced by more convenient and useful perspectives.

I had assumed that the incoming beliefs about the relationship of caring and teaching brought by my students to their field place-ment experiences—the gentle smiles and warm hugs they had seen on countless television commercials and dreamed of offering to children themselves one day—would be poorly aligned with the realities of life in classrooms with young children. The purpose of the second part of this study, then, was to learn more about the specific ways in which the students' initial understandings of caring were challenged and changed during the course of their field placement period. I was particularly interested in exploring the ways that my students resolved the dilemmas and tensions they encountered when their preconceptions about the relationship between caring and teaching proved inadequate.

Naturally, my desire was that these reconsiderations would enable the preservice teachers to move forward into more nuanced understandings that would reflect professional maturation. To use Deweyan terms (Dewey, 1938), I hoped the students' field placements would be an educative experience. However, the literature foretold of other possible outcomes. The research cited earlier indicating the strong influence of biography and previous experience would suggest that student teaching is often a non-educative experience (Dewey, 1938), allowing preservice teachers' beliefs and preconceptions to remain unchanged. On the other hand, the research highlighting the ease with which students slide into traditional and rigid pedagogies during the field placement experience would identify student teaching as a potentially miseducative experience.

So, despite my initial optimism about the students' growth and development, I knew that the outcomes of the students' reflections on and reconsiderations of the relationship of caring and teaching would cover a wide spectrum of possibility. Deeper knowledge of this dimension of the students' professional preparation will allow teacher educators to better support students during the transitions and professional instability that accompany field placement experiences and will give us opportunities to ensure that preservice teachers negotiate their challenges in ways that allow them to maintain a meaningful and thoughtful commitment to caring teaching.

My interest in my preservice teachers' initial attempts to enact caring teaching was also fueled by some nagging concerns that I harbored about the challenges of caring teaching. Because of the prevalence of the warm smiles and gentle hugs view of elementary schoolteachers' professional lives, there exists a sense that caring teaching is natural and easy. The research literature offers documentation of the joy and pleasure of teaching children. For example, Lortie found caring relationships with students to be a significant source of professional satisfaction for teachers, one of the "psychic rewards" of a career in education (Lortie, 1975, p. 104).

Nias (1989) quotes a teacher who reinforces Lortie's position, highlighting the mutuality of the student-teacher relationship: the teacher says, "Don't think I'm the one who's doing all the giving . . . . I know that by the end of the day several people will have shown that they love me" (Nias, 1989, p. 87). Similarly, Hargreaves (1994) notes that many teachers elected to enter the profession because of a strong commitment to caring for children and considered caring relationships with children to be a significant source of job satisfaction throughout their careers.

However, a commitment to caring has also been positioned as a potential source of difficulty for teachers, and this was my concern. As Robin Leavitt (1994) points out, at times even the most committed teacher's capacities for ongoing caregiving are exhausted due to the inherently unequal nature of a caring teacher-student relationship. The child's understandably limited ability to contribute to the maintenance and sustenance of this caring relation can lead to emotional strain, anger, and alienation for the teacher. When teachers become burdened in this way, their caring feelings are transformed into "emotional labor—the publicly observable management of feelings sold for a wage" (Leavitt, 1994, p. 61).

Even under favorable circumstances, caring for students can be demanding and exasperating. Sandra Acker describes the frazzled state of a primary teacher after a particularly long day: "She loves the class, she says, though she could tear her hair out" (Acker, 1995, p. 26). Because of strong feelings of commitment and responsibility, teachers invest enormous amounts of time and energy in their caring relations with their students (Nias, 1989; Hargreaves, 1994). Prone to perfectionism, many caring teachers face feelings of frustration and guilt when they are unable to meet fully all the needs of their students (Hargreaves, 1994; Hargreaves & Tucker, 1991), thereby making themselves vulnerable to professional burn-out.

Another reason I hoped to find out more about my preservice teachers' first experiences with caring for children in public elementary school settings was to come to understand the professional challenges they encountered and to explore their strategies for managing the challenges associated with caring teaching. Doing so will enable us to develop teacher education strategies that will prepare novice teachers both to draw upon the pedagogical power of caring and to avoid succumbing to the burn-out and exhaustion that might accompany a commitment to caring teaching; it is important that our re/visioned care-centered approaches to teacher education prepare students for the challenges they can realistically expect to encounter.

Chapter 4

Initial Understandings of Caring Teaching

Several recent textbooks have been developed for use in courses aimed at preparing novice teachers to create classrooms and professional identities centered around caring relationships with children. These textbooks, such as Charney's *Teaching Children to Care* (1992), and Dalton & Watson's *Among Friends: Classrooms Where Caring and Learning Prevail* (1997), focus on classroom processes and practices, offering strategies for creating caring communities in classrooms. To use Dunkin and Biddle's (1974) terminology, these texts focus on process variables—teacher behaviors and student behaviors in classroom contexts. Little or no attention is paid to the role of what Dunkin and Biddle refer to as presage variables—teacher background, beliefs, values, experiences and so on—in the development of care-centered teaching practices.

However, preservice teachers do not enter their professional preparation empty-handed. Thanks to the apprenticeship of observation (Lortie, 1975), these individuals bring with them images and understandings of teaching that will shape their nascent practices. Preservice teachers begin their teacher education experiences with preconceived, atheoretical ideas of the relationship of teaching and caring, ideas which reverberate throughout the teachers' initial forays into classroom life (McLaughlin, 1991; Tabachnick & Zeichner, 1984).

In this chapter I share the results of a recent study of a group of preservice elementary teachers in which I examined the understandings of the role of caring in educational contexts brought by these novices to their first field placement experiences. Rather than attending to process variables—the teachers' emergent practices—I focused upon presage variables—the teachers' beliefs and understandings—and the teachers' reflections on their classroom experiences. As Cole & Knowles's work would suggest (Cole & Knowles, 1993) and as I feared, I found that my students' conceptions of the relationship between teaching and caring were underdeveloped and limited.

Beliefs about caring and teaching

In the students' ejournal considerations of caring, slogan-eering occasionally stood in place of genuine insight. For Ariel[1], "a caring teacher is one who is truly devoted to improving and educating fellow members of the human race," whereas Andi notes "I care for every child because I know they hold the future for us." The students had only just begun their field placements when they wrote these first reflections; they drew on idealized images of teaching they'd developed over the years rather than on real experience with children in classrooms.

For most of the students, caring and teaching were inextricably linked. It was difficult for some of them to separate the two constructs. Because they conflated caring and teaching, the students were predisposed to see evidence of caring in their cooperating teachers' practices. Many of the students had little difficulty; their ejournals were rich with stories of relationships attended to and nourished through caring teaching. However, some of the students were not so fortunate, spending field placement time in classrooms where slow children were given nicknames like "Flash" or "the human lump," and where teachers consciously decided not to allow themselves to get attached to the children.

Even when faced with practices that appeared to demonstrate a marked absence of caring, however, the students worked hard

---

[1]The names of the preservice teachers, their students, their cooperating teachers, and their field placement school sites have been changed to protect their anonymity.

to find ways to see those practices as examples of caring teaching. For example, Rosita writes:

> The environment was cluttered and there were posters that were falling down; I took this to be some form of caring. . . . The relationship between teacher and student was interesting. I never saw her hug a child, or say good morning. She put children in time out quite often. . . . I have looked very hard for the caring relationship between teacher and student, it must be what they call tough love. I know she cares for her students, I need to figure it out for myself.

Though it clearly caused some cognitive dissonance for the students—particularly Rosita, quoted above—no one was willing to question the automatic connection of teaching and caring or to interrogate the underlying assumptions of their cooperating teachers' practices.

At the start of the semester, Kay wrote: "One of my initial reasons for wanting to become a teacher is because I care so much about children. I absolutely love them!" Echoing this sentiment, Leigh wrote, "Caring is a characteristic that I think all students who want to be teachers possess. It comes easy for them." These entries capture several important and commonly-held aspects of the student teachers' understandings of caring: essentialism, oversimplification, and idealism.

Essentialism

Discussing caring, Andi asserted, "I think that caring for a student comes naturally," and Mary stated, "I think a caring teacher cares for each child as a student and as a person. When the caring is genuine, it is as natural as it should be." A surprisingly large number of the student teachers in the cohort believed that both caring and teaching are rooted in instinct; phrases like "second nature," "a gift," "completely instinctive," and "natural talent" peppered all of the students' ejournals.

That caring is considered an essentialist trait is not surprising; many widely held and long-standing notions such as maternal instinct and motherly love indicate the prevalence of this belief system (Thurer, 1991). What is surprising, though, is that students in a teacher education program could be so strongly committed to an essentialist viewpoint on teaching. Given that their degree program had been specifically designed to teach people to become teachers and to support them in the process, it seems that the students would think of teaching as a skill or an art that can be taught and learned, and not a gift or a personality trait. But the belief that being a teacher is "natural" was pervasive among the students.

Halfway through her field placement experience, Roberta experienced a professional and personal crisis directly caused by this essentialist belief. She wrote:

> Over the past month, maybe a little less, I thought that I was not cut out to be a teacher. I thought that I did not have enough of the qualities to be a good teacher. . . . As you might expect, my parents freaked out. And that is putting it lightly, very. They were right, I have always wanted to be a teacher as long as I can remember. I have always adored children and I have a great rapport with them. Just recently I have doubted everything in myself and really struggled to find what it takes to teach.

Roberta got stuck in a trap set by an essentialist understanding of teaching: being a teacher is a natural instinct, and either you have it or you don't. And, since teaching is natural, then it should be easy. If you are working hard at it, or if you feel like you're failing at it, then you probably don't have that natural instinct and should get out of the profession.

Barbie avoided that trap by successfully balancing strongly held essentialist beliefs—"I have always thought it was just something natural that God had given me, a talent for working with kids"—with an understanding of the role of hard work in becoming a caring teacher—"Then I realized that you have to refine that talent to be able to teach those children." This belief that time and effort are central requirements of caring teaching ran counter to the essentialist position, and was shared by several of the students:

If you put time, effort, and some caring into it, students can definitely benefit. (Andi)
I think that a teacher that is willing to put that much time and effort to make sure that her students are learning, yet having fun in the process, exemplifies a caring teacher. (Barbie)

A caring teacher has many facets. A caring teacher will take time to show his/her students this by engaging themselves in the students' lives. . . . The teacher makes a valiant effort to understand their students and show their interest in them individually. (Devry)

Just as these students balanced their essentialist beliefs with an awareness of the value of hard work, Ariel balanced her essentialist beliefs about being a caring teacher with an almost existential understanding of the power of commitment and choice, writing:

If I did not care about my students' retention, comprehension, or enjoyment, teaching would be simple. I could look at the state curriculum, pass out worksheets, assign textbook pages, grade [them], and send them on their way. However, there is something deep inside me that will not let me. Call it my conscience, my heart, my instinct, or my nature. All of these add up to form a tremendous commitment to my students.

Ariel's emphatic insistence on thinking about what she is doing with her students and taking responsibility for their experiences evokes Maxine Greene's (1973) views on teaching:

As people concerned with education, we are inescapably caught up in the pursuit of the worthwhile. . . . We can easily say that we are assigned to teach our students to learn how to think intelligently and critically, to realize their potential, to appreciate everwidening areas of experience. We can easily say that we want to help students develop desirable states of mind. But everyone who teaches knows that such general declarations have little meaning in the day-to-day life of the classroom. The teacher is concerned with specific actions, concrete decisions. Functioning intentionally with particular children in particular situations, he has to decide what to do to focus on worthwhile achievement. (Greene, 1973, p. 220)

Roberta, too, spoke to the issues of commitment and consciousness in caring teaching, realizing "that we need to be very
aware of the power we hold over these children." She went on to
assert:

> Each time a teacher speaks to or with a child, part of a relationship
> is built. A teacher has to be very conscious about what she is saying at
> all times. A teacher can break down a child's confidence. On the other
> hand, a teacher can take this opportunity to show how much she cares
> for the child.

Echoing Maxine Greene's call for a sense of "wide-awakeness"
(Greene 1978, p. 42) in teaching, Roberta insisted that caring
teachers must remember their obligation to maintain an engaged
awareness of their relationships with and responsibility to the
children in their classrooms. This stance contradicts — or perhaps
balances — Roberta's strong essentialist beliefs that were discussed
previously.

The tensions and contradictions within Roberta's conceptions
of teaching are not surprising. Teaching is a rich and complicated
undertaking; even experienced teachers find contradiction,
tension, and inconsistency to be inescapable facets of their work
(Ayers, 1993). Furthermore, for these students this placement is a
time of transition; they are transforming themselves from college
kids to elementary school teachers. The apparent disjuncture
between Roberta's sophisticated understandings of caring
teaching and her simple essentialist beliefs about the natural
instincts contributing to both caring and teaching may be an
inevitable by-product of this transition.

Oversimplification

Because the image of the caring teacher is so prevalent in our
culture, it was easy for the students to fall into overly simple
understandings of what it meant to teach with care. Roberta exemplifies this phenomenon, writing "A caring teacher has to have
love, love, and more love for children." Teaching, a profoundly
complex endeavor, was often reduced by the students to mirror
the flat representations of "typical" teachers found on television

commercials, greeting cards, magazine advertisements, and in the movies. Further, because the pedagogical aspects of teacherly life still seemed mysterious and remote to them, the students in my cohort concentrated instead on aspects of teaching that were more tangible and immediate: behaviors and interactional styles.

Many students were gentle smilers and warm huggers and focused on the personal in their ejournal entries, centering their beliefs about the relationship of teaching and caring in their emotions. The tendency to view caring as a personality trait, one necessary to be a good teacher, is common among teachers (Nias, 1989). Other students focused on the global, emphasizing the contribution of caring teaching not only to the children involved, but to the world in general. An example of this perspective comes from Mary's ejournal: "My goal is to care for all children for the special individuals they are and for what they have to share with the world."

Along similar lines, for many of the students caring meant being nice. Maria asserted that "a caring teacher was one who is kind, loving, patient and one who never raises his/her voice at the students." Kay chose teaching as her profession because of the opportunities it appeared to provide for engaging in nice interactions: "I decided I wanted to be an elementary school teacher because, at that age, most—if not all—of the kids love their teacher. I do not think I could deal with a classroom full of students who did not like me."

Due in part to portrayals of teachers in popular culture (Freedman, 1999; Joseph & Burnaford, 1994; Weber & Mitchell, 1995) and in part to deeply ingrained and gendered stereotypes of elementary school teaching as women's work (Acker, 1999; Biklen, 1992, 1995; Freedman, 1990; Grumet, 1988), teaching appears inextricably linked with a particular constellation of affective traits. Through their work with preservice primary teachers in Britain, Burgess & Carter (1992) identified a widely-shared set of understandings which they have called "the Mumsy discourse." The Mumsy discourse explicitly links teaching young children both with images of idealized, middle class mothering and with "socially approved feminine virtues such as 'caring' and nurturance" (Burgess & Carter, 1992, p. 353).

Along lines similar to the Mumsy discourse, Beth Swadener (1992) coined the phrase "the hegemony of nice" to describe this phenomenon; the term captures the strength and the breadth of the belief that elementary teachers are nice, friendly, warm, kind, gentle and so on (Nias, 1989). This linkage of teaching and "nice" persisted as my students wrestled with their emerging profes-sional identities.

The students' tendency to oversimplify further presents itself in their desire to reduce a complex, organic, professional experience into two tidy and mutually exclusive categories: teachers are either nice or not nice. Devry wonders "if students ultimately respond better to a compassionate, fun teacher compared to a stiff, demanding one?"; Barbie believes "there is a huge difference between being an unbiased professional and a caring teacher. It is very hard to know the correct time to assume each role." Though some students struggled to find a balancing point, these ejournal entries indicate that students were drawing a line in the sand: as a teacher one is either professional, unbiased, and unfeeling OR compassionate, fun, and caring.

In the sense of caring shared by most of the students in the cohort, caring was a feeling. Caring teachers display a particular set of behaviors and engage with children in a particular manner: the gentle smiles and warms hugs that Rogers (1994, p. 33) described. Not only were my students unable to see caring as a moral and intellectual relation, but they were very narrow in the range of emotions and behaviors they associated with caring teaching. Other possible styles of caring teacher-student inter-action that might look and sound different from the gentle smiles and warm hugs prized by my students (see Eaker-Rich & Van Galen, 1996, and Noblit, 1993 for examples) were discussed in the students' ejournals only occasionally. For instance, Barbie wrote:

> I've learned that caring doesn't mean that you are nice to someone just for the sake of being nice. I've learned that caring is also being hard on someone because you know that they can do better, or challenging

someone because you want them to learn. Caring involves truly wanting them to succeed.

Barbie rejects the idea of caring as simply being nice in favor of a more sophisticated and mature notion of caring.

Other students highlighted one particular aspect of being nice, considering service and helping to be central features of caring teaching. Leigh stated:

> Caring can be shown in the classroom in a variety of ways and I will mention a few that I have seen this week. Getting a bag for a student who has lost a tooth, delegating roles for students to be for the day, allowing students to make choices for certain activities, calling on students who do not have their hands raised and helping them along with the problem . . . and not being upset that you cannot get any work done at your desk because students are continually coming up to you with tons of questions.

Echoing Leigh's beliefs, Thuy wrote: "An educator must take pleasure in dedicating his or her life to serving children." The deep connection of teaching to stereotypically feminine behaviors and images is obvious in these statements. Eager to please and eager to succeed, the students exhibited a tendency to play it safe, rarely straying from the well-known understandings and representations of the "typical" elementary school teacher.

Idealism

Weinstein argues that "a vision of teaching that emphasizes affective dimensions may be partly responsible for prospective teachers' unrealistic optimism" (Weinstein, 1990, p. 280); this appears to have been true for the students in this study. Not only were their journal entries rich with examples of their belief in the centrality of affect in caring teaching, but the students' initial journal entries were also overflowing with idealistic descriptions of caring teaching. These entries showcased their optimism and hope for their lives in the profession while simultaneously reflecting their lack of real-world experience in classrooms.

Patience, devotion, and love feature prominently in these early entries. For example, Roberta wrote:

> I know what kind of caring teacher I want to be. I want to have an endless, deep love for children that lasts through the years. I do not want it to diminish as I get older. Also, I want to be very patient with everyone, even the most difficult child.

These idealized, romantic notions were clearly rooted in the students' aspirations and images of the teachers they hoped to become. Some of the students painted detailed portraits of their future selves in their ejournal entries, each with a different emphasis or focus. Mark, for example, centered his image of an ideal teacher on affective issues when he wrote:

> A caring teacher . . . would be one to care about the children's personal life and interests. This teacher should be available for the child in any capacity and should never turn a deaf ear on a child's problem or concern. He or she should also help the child meet his or her potential in all areas of school and help them refine/understand their personal interests. A caring teacher should be quick to praise and never ridicule a student in front of others. Discipline should be fair and enforced in a timely manner. Caring encompasses a wide range of activities and should never be forgotten or dismissed.

Ariel, on the other hand, centered her description on pedagogical issues:

> Teachers who care want their students to enjoy learning. Caring means going to great lengths to create lesson plans, find manipulatives, learn individual styles and try to make stations for the different types [of students]. Caring means specifically tailoring assignments to individual classes, taking time to assess each student, staying late to tutor. Caring in teaching practices is scrapping a magnificent unit for the class that does not understand or does not enjoy it and starting fresh.

Each student equated caring with his or her personal standards of good teaching practices. This was almost invisible because the majority of the students' held a shared set of beliefs and values about what would constitute "good teaching." This shared stance, evident in Mark's and Ariel's ejournal entries quoted above, was in all likelihood a product of the students' shared experiences moving through their education and methods coursework as a cohort—all the students heard the same things from the same sources.

My preservice teachers had been dreaming of a teaching career since they were elementary school children themselves and were finally seeing that dream come to fruition. Their idealistic and romantic notions about teaching and caring are rooted in these dreams (Bullough & Stokes, 1994). At this point in their professional preparation, the students were hesitant to push their thinking on caring and its role in teaching. Saddled with a demanding courseload and overwhelmed by the enormous responsibility that accompanies being accountable to children in a classroom setting, the students were content to hold onto their dream-like images of caring teaching.

As I had expected, my students were indeed gentle smilers and warm huggers—these were the preconceptions they brought to the course. And, as the research predicted, these prior beliefs about the nature of caring teaching and the relationship between caring and teaching were hard to shake (Kagan, 1992). Within the context of the classroom organization and management course— through readings, lectures, class discussions, and a range of hands-on activities—I attempted to present more sophisticated conceptions of caring than those brought by the students to my classroom.

For example, together we explored Noddings's (1984) idea that caring is a moral choice and an intellectual act rather than a personality trait, and examined my notion that caring relation-ships play a central role in children's cognitive growth and should be thought of as more than just a vehicle for enhancing children's self-esteem and for enabling pleasant exchanges in the classroom (Goldstein, 1999). I also attempted to use the ejournals as a site for challenging and enhancing the students' partial understandings of caring in the context of a one-on-one dialogue exchange.

However, just as Kagan (1992) found, my efforts and the ideas I offered appeared to have little impact on the students' thinking or their practices.

But, as Cole & Knowles's (1993) research would suggest, the students would not remain untouched by their field experiences. The gentle smiles and warm hugs view of caring that had brought them into the teaching profession and sustained them through some of the earlier, easier parts of their field placement period was challenged as the students spent more time in their school sites and took on increasing responsibility in their placement classrooms. In the next chapter, I discuss the dilemmas my preservice teachers encountered as they attempted to enact their gentle smiles and warm hugs views of caring in their placement classrooms.

Chapter 5

Challenges Enacting
Caring Teaching

This chapter follows my preservice teachers into their field place-ment classrooms, exploring the ways in which their preconceived understandings of caring teaching, described in detail in chapter 4, played out as they engaged in their first long-term teaching experiences.

In the preservice teachers' preconceptions, caring was seen as natural and easy; caring teachers were kind, loving, patient, and soft-spoken. My preservice teacher education students were con-fident and optimistic about their ability to teach with care. However, once their field placements were in full swing, they found themselves in a zone of discomfort and dis-equilibrium, struggling with issues related to establishing their professional identity, coping with the tensions between caring and loss, and clarifying their understandings of parent-teacher-child relation-ships. Confronting these challenges to their initial gentle smiles and warm hugs understandings of caring teaching, my preservice teachers were poised at a threshold of professional possibility: their perspectives were likely to change as a result of their field placements, but in what ways?

Hollingsworth insists that teacher educators "should come to understand the incoming beliefs of [their] students" (Hollings-worth, 1989, p. 161). I support this belief. However, my work in this study suggests that understanding students' incoming beliefs is only a first step. Teacher educators must also attend carefully to the ways that those beliefs are challenged or reinforced during the students' field placement experiences. In this chapter, I discuss the shifts and changes—some for the better, some for the worse, and some still unclear—in the preservice teachers' beliefs about the relationship of caring and teaching that occurred during their first field placement experience.

Enacting caring teaching

Once their placement experiences were well underway, my preservice teachers were forced to confront the complexities of teacherly caring and to begin to re-shape the contours of their previously-held beliefs. The students often struggled to reconcile their idealized understandings of caring teaching with the realities of the profession as they were faced with a range of practical dilemmas that required a more sophisticated and complicated sense of the relationship of teaching and caring than that offered by their gentle smiles and warm hugs view. As the students realized that their initial preconceptions about caring and teaching were inadequate to explain the complexity of what they were witnessing and experiencing in their field placement classrooms, they were cast into a zone of disequilibrium, discomfort, and confusion.

The preservice teachers' ejournal entries reflected their uncertainty and struggle. Analysis of the students' ejournal entries revealed that their most significant dilemmas involved establishing their professional identities as caring teachers, coping with the teachers' fundamental, inherent challenge of caring deeply for children who will only be "yours" for a limited period of time, and negotiating their understandings of the relationships between caring teachers and their pupils' parents. Confronted by these challenges, the students began to reconsider their initial beliefs and reshape their thinking about the interactions of caring and teaching.

In response to each of these three dilemmas, however, the students' understandings shifted in different ways. In the case of dilemmas about caring and professional identity, the students appeared to be in the early stages of disequilibrium. I found the students wrestling with these issues throughout their placement period, but at the conclusion of the study the directions in which they might be moving as they resolved their struggles remained unclear. With the dilemmas relating to the tensions between caring and loss, however, the students appeared to make changes in their thinking that reflected increasing professional maturity.

And in the case of the challenges linked to developing caring parent-teacher-child relationships, the students appeared to abandon their idealistic and simple initial conceptions in favor of new beliefs and attitudes that were narrow, judgmental, and troubling to me as a teacher educator.

Caring and professional identity

Beginning to establish a professional sense of self is a central educational goal of the students' first field placement. One challenge many of the students faced as they embarked on this journey of self-definition was discarding worn-out metaphors they had previously used when imagining themselves as caring teachers. For example, during her first week in her classroom placement, Kay found herself "having a hard time separating the baby-sitting world and the teaching world." Kay automatically drew upon previously established patterns of caring interaction with children but found them to be inadequate and inappropriate within the context of a classroom: she realized the chasm separating baby-sitting from teaching.

Like Kay, other students confronted the limitations of their working metaphors for caring teaching. Mark worried that his goal of "being viewed [by the students] as a good friend when you are also their teacher" was causing him to be too easy on the students. Barbie wrestled with her "natural instinct to want to mother the children instead of teach them," finding, like Kay and Mark, that although a teaching relation is rooted in caring, it is distinctly unlike other caring relations between children and adults.

Lortie (1975) described in great detail the ways that biography plays a role in teachers' development of their professional self-images: models and beliefs that take hold in childhood are internalized and remain strongly influential throughout pre-service teachers' preparation and induction. The images of teaching held by my students quoted above—baby-sitter, good friend, and mother—are, in all likelihood, images deeply rooted in the students' life histories. For example, it seems that Barbie had strong connections with Burgess & Carter's (1992) "Mumsy discourse," a way of thinking which links teaching young children both with caring and with images of idealized, white middle-class mothering.

As others have argued, central images of practice (Connelly & Clandinin, 1988) and other teaching metaphors (Bullough, 1991; Cole & Knowles, 1993) are deeply seeded and profoundly powerful. Negotiating the transmutation from baby-sitter /friend/mother, the images most prevalent among my students, to teacher/authority figure was a key challenge facing these students as they worked on developing their professional identities. A particularly complex aspect of this process involved the establishment and maintenance of comfortable interpersonal relationships with the students in their classes.

After attending one of her students' weekend soccer games, Barbie wrote:

> I think it's important to show children that you love and care for them and you support them in all their endeavors (not just academia). At first I wondered if this broke the professionalism of being a teacher (i.e., keeping the relationship confined strictly to between the walls of the school). The more that I have thought about it, I truly believe that teaching is caring about individuals and when you are for someone as a human being you don't set limits on when and where you are for them.

Barbie concluded that her personal understanding of profes-sionalism left room for certain levels of extracurricular intimacy and relationship. Devry, on the other hand, created boundaries for appropriate professional conduct that were much tighter than Barbie's. Her boundary-setting experience happened during the writing of one of her ejournal entries. Devry's decision-making process is revealed here:

> One student in particular, [a child] that I have connected with and really like, wants to hold my hand, especially while walking in line. Is this appropriate to do?. . . . When I think about it, I do not see any harm in it, except that it might lessen the authority figure [image/status] that a teacher needs to have. Any thoughts about this? I am a strong believer in showing my students affection though. I find I give out lots of hugs. The dilemma I have is knowing where to draw the line, from a hug to holding their hands. The more I think about it, the more it seems too much, holding the student's hand. I already feel somewhat uncomfortable when this particular student wants to hold my hand.

Devry begins by saying she likes the child and sees no real harm in holding his hand; three lines later Devry has come to the opposite conclusion, stating that she has felt uncomfortable with the child's desire and doesn't want to hold hands. Using her reflective journal to scaffold herself as she reorganizes her schema for teacherly caring, Devry worked toward resolution of a professional dilemma.

Underlying the students' concern for establishing boundaries is a broader and more complicated professional identity issue: the need to negotiate a stance with regard to legitimate authority and teacherly caring. The dilemmas related to balancing caring and control are challenging even for experienced teachers (Hargreaves, 1994). Managing the tension between being nice and having authority is an essential dilemma faced by novice teachers as they experience their first extended stay in a classroom. As McLaughlin described it, preservice teachers often find that "their attempts to care may conflict with their hope of assuming an authoritative professional stance" (McLaughlin, 1991, p. 182).

My students spent a good deal of time considering this dilemma: it was difficult for them to envision ways to smile gently, hug warmly, and still maintain control of their classrooms. Often, students saw caring and authority laid out in a simple either/or dichotomy. For example, in describing her cooperating teacher, Thuy stated: "She is not only an educator, but also a caregiver." Thuy felt her cooperating teacher to be noteworthy because she managed to be *not only* an educator, *but also* a caregiver, as if these were usually two mutually exclusive options.

Along similar lines, Devry wondered "if students ultimately respond better to a compassionate, fun teacher compared to a stiff, demanding one?" and Barbie believed "there is a huge difference between being an unbiased professional and a caring teacher. It is very hard to know the correct time to assume each role." In the eyes of these novice teachers, one is either professional, unbiased, and unfeeling OR compassionate, fun, and caring.

At other times, students in my cohort veered away from this tendency toward oversimplification and stark either/or dualisms and instead wrestled with a more sophisticated and nuanced understanding of the tension between authority and caring. These ejournal entries capture the complexity and fluidity that are a daily reality in the lives of classroom teachers. Kate stated, "I think that a major dilemma of teaching is finding a balance between necessary discipline and showing that you care for your students." Likewise, Devry mused, "I have always wondered how as a teacher to be caring yet firm and disciplined with the class."

Experienced teachers have a range of ways to manage these dilemmas (McLaughlin, 1991). Kay's cooperating teacher, for example, offered her advice that echoes the old "don't smile till Christmas" adage: Kay wrote, "I really wanted the kids to like me, but Mrs. Lester kept telling me that it is important to first demand respect and liking will come with it." Devry's cooperating teacher, on the other hand, modeled a working balance between caring and authority that seemed more rooted in joy and connection with the children than in demanding respect from the children. Devry founds that watching her cooperating teacher led her to believe that "teachers can have a great time with their students and still be the authority."

After asserting her authority and disciplining students for the first time, Andi reflected on the working balance she was able to establish that day, and wrote: "I felt very good because taking away their [reward sticker] stars made me feel like I was being a 'mean' person, but I was actually doing my job." Andi wrestled with the ways that feeling good, feeling like she was being mean, and "actually doing [her] job" folded back upon each other, and she attempted to reconcile the conflicting and complex inter-actions among these feelings and responsibilities and under-standings.

In general, the students positioned being nice and being authoritative in opposition to one another. George Noblit (1993) offers an interpretation of the tension between niceness and authority that transforms the terrain of this essential dilemma. Noblit asserts that caring in classrooms is not about finding a balance between exerting teacherly authority and demonstrating teacherly nurturance; instead, caring "is about the ethical use of power" (Noblit, 1993, p. 24). Repositioning the dilemma in this manner offers a way to think about caring and authority that skirts the either/or tension that plagued my students. Instead, Noblit's view encourages the development of a sense of teacherly responsibility and consciousness and is likely to strengthen novices' professional identities.

In the ejournal entries relating to the establishment of professional identity, I found my students in a state of flux. My preservice teachers realized the limitations of their previous metaphors of caring teaching, faced the complex landscape of student-teacher relationships, and questioned the relationship between caring and authority. The students had begun the process of wrestling with the challenges before them, but none of them had taken great strides toward the resolution of their dilemmas.

At the conclusion of this study it was impossible to determine how the students' professional identities as caring teachers would come to be characterized. Letting go of inadequate prior conceptions of teaching is only a benefit to preservice teachers if the new conceptions and metaphors they adopt are fuller and richer than the ones left behind. With ample support during their student teaching semester and in their induction year, these novices might develop professional identities rooted in responsible and thoughtful caring; at the end of the study it was too early to tell.

Caring and loss

The caring relationships with pupils that each of the students worked hard to establish and to nurture were a source of joy, pride, fulfillment, and validation for them. However, like all caring relationships, these close connections made the students vulnerable to hurt and heartache. As Ariel wrote: "It hurts to care. However, I couldn't imagine not caring about my students for a second. After this week, I have realized my own version of an old cliché: It's better to have cared and lost, then not to have cared at all."

My preservice teachers' first encounters with these painful losses occurred when children in their placement classrooms moved away during the students' time in the field. The students were shocked at the depth and intensity of their sadness at the loss of a teacherly relationship. Often, their reflections contained the seeds of meaningful personal growth. The first time Ariel had a pupil move away (a classroom experience she later called "the part of teaching I hate"), for example, she coped with her sadness in a way that gave her great strength when she faced this situation again at later points in her field placement:

> Did I give her a hug the last time I saw her? Did I have to correct her or was it just a day of smiles? How will she remember me? Will she remember me? Out of the questions and emotions came some comfort from newfound wisdom. No one knows how long one will have a student. There is no safety in assuming the child you have today will be there tomorrow. Therefore, every day must be treated as though you'll never see that child again. That means there's never too much time for hugging, smiling, encouraging. The exciting things you put off tomorrow may never be realized. The child you put off until tomorrow may not be there the next day to explain your reactions or emotions. You must invest today as if there is no tomorrow.

Ariel's journal entry refers directly to "newfound wisdom" garnered through experience: her thinking about the essential nature of caring teaching was changed and her prior conceptions of teaching were discarded as a result of "losing" a child.

The preservice teachers' sense of loss was particularly acute when they came to the end of their field placements. Unlike the specific and localized feelings of loss that accompanied the departure of individual children from their classes, these feelings of loss were global and immense. All of the preservice teachers were affected to one degree or another, and their ejournals were filled with tales of overwhelming feelings. Describing her last day with her children, Halina wrote: "Tears came to my eyes and, believe me, I had to make a huge effort not to cry . . ., I had such a lump in my throat. I told them I wasn't feeling well, which was the truth anyway."

Halina's emotional response surprised neither her nor us; she felt deeply connected to her children and many of her ejournal entries were rich with feeling. However, there were other students for whom the intensity of their response to leaving their placement classrooms was unexpected. For example, Maria reported:

> I did not think I would be this sad about having to end my internship until Wednesday morning when Ms. Ziffle [her cooperating teacher] informed the children that Thursday was going to be my last day with them. The choice of words she used in telling the students and the atmosphere it provided brought sadness to my heart and made my eyes water. I knew at that moment it was going to be difficult for me to say my good-byes on Thursday without crying. Well sure enough, as I was telling the students how and why they were special to me, tears rolled down my cheeks as they are now as I write this entry. I could not believe I cried! I never cry! But just the fact that I was not going to see these sweet, cute faces almost every day anymore, made me truly sad.

Maria could not believe the sadness she experienced at the end of her placement. She had held an image of herself as someone who never cried and had imagined a world of teaching that contained far less discomfort and emotion than the world she encountered. As a result of her experience in Mrs. Ziffle's first grade classroom, Maria was forced to think differently about herself and about the relationship of caring and teaching.

These feelings of loss are inevitable, a standard part of a teacher's experience. At the conclusion of my stay in Martha George's classroom, I felt the familiar sense of heartache and loss that accompanies the end of the school year, and I reflected on the experience (Goldstein, 1997, pp. 153-4):

> Teachers enter into [these] relationships knowing full well they will not last. Each year, the cycle of teacherly love plays itself out in classrooms. Children arrive, relationships grow and blossom. In June the gorgeous blossoms are picked while in full bloom. The end of the school year is a difficult time . . . the severing of mutual attachment is painful.

Nelson, too, has documented the pain teachers feel when separating from their students at year's end; she quotes one teacher as saying, "It is very hard. You feel like you're losing a part of you" (Nelson, 1994, p. 199). Along similar lines, Bullough & Knowles (1991) tell the story of a teacher who looks at her students in the last week of school and thinks "I'm never going to see these kids again. I've been busting my [rear end] to connect with them, and I'm never going to see them again . . . . This is going to rip me apart" (Bullough & Knowles, 1991, p. 137).

Vickie, my teaching assistant and the students' fieldwork supervisor, and I attempted to prepare the students for this painful separation, recalling our own years as elementary teachers and sharing our experiences of hardship and loss at the end of the year. Students appeared to have gotten the message.

Picking up on my teaching stories, Devry asked, "How did you handle the last day of each year with your students? Knowing you as I do, I am sure you have shed a few tears on the last day of class!" Along similar lines, Barbie wrote: "I know that it will just kill me as a teacher to say good-bye after spending such quality time for a whole year with them. I feel as if they were my own children after just a semester of half days!" However, both we and the students learned that loss of this kind is hard to know fully until it has been experienced first-hand.

Becoming involved in mutually caring relationships with students is one of the perks of teaching (Hargreaves, 1994; Niao,

1989); my students rushed headlong into these relationships and found them deeply satisfying. I would contend that our preservice teachers had fallen in "teacherly love" with their students (Goldstein, 1997, p. 98). Characterized, like other forms of love, by commitment, intimacy and passion (Sternberg, 1988a), yet constrained by the structures of the institution of schooling, teacherly love is a unique, specific form of love familiar to many educators. Teacherly love is unlike other forms of love, I argue, in that it is shaped by the academic calendar, by the contours of pedagogical relationships, and by the boundaries of professional responsibility.

Unaware of the distinct parameters of teacherly love and apparently acting on the belief that caring was monolithic, the same regardless of the relational context, our students bonded with their children just as they had bonded in their prior significant relationships. But then, at the end of their field placement period, the students found their implicit working definition of a caring relationship—a definition rooted in constancy and duration over time, a definition that had served them well in the past—inadequate to capture the challenges specific to teacherly caring.

The students' pain at separating from their children helped them realize that caring teaching was more complex and multi-faceted than they had suspected. Their ejournal entries indicate that the preservice teachers' understandings of teacherly caring were enhanced and enriched by the combination of experience and reflection provided by their classroom placements and the accompanying journaling assignments. In the case of this particular facet of their teacherly lives, the students' initial conceptions of caring teaching were slowly being replaced by an understanding that was richer, fuller, and more realistic. The preservice teachers' struggles with this particular professional dilemma appears to have led to a change for the better.

Caring and parent-teacher-child relationships

The students quickly realized that teachers engage not only with individual children, but also with the significant adults in those children's lives. Developing and negotiating relationships with parents is a particularly sensitive and complex facet of a teacher's professional responsibility (Barbour, 1996; Bredekamp & Copple, 1997; Bronfenbrenner, 1974; Coleman & Churchill, 1997; Epstein, 1988; Hoover-Dempsey, Bassler & Brissie, 1985; Moles, 1982; Powell & Diamond, 1995), and the preservice teachers in the study struggled with this challenge.

As with their reading of niceness and authority discussed earlier, the preservice teachers tended to group parents into two clear-cut categories: good parents and bad parents. As the students encountered the value-laden complexity of parent-child-teacher relations, however, simple categories and understandings were inadequate. Yet the preservice teachers appeared to cling more tightly than ever to that good parent/bad parent binary, developing potentially troublesome understandings of the boundaries of teacherly responsibility and showcasing unsettling attitudes toward parents.

The students understood caring for their pupils to be one of their central responsibilities as teachers. Because of this, they felt a great deal of protective loyalty toward the youngsters in their classes. As a result, the students often questioned their children's parents' judgment, and even positioned themselves in opposition to the parents on occasion. The tensions between teachers and parents have been well-documented (Biklen, 1992; Goldstein, 1998a; Grumet, 1988; Levin, 1987; Lightfoot, 1977; McPherson, 1972; Ribbens, 1993); my students appear to have been quick studies, learning these "typical" teacherly responses with ease.

Often the students were concerned that their children's parents were underinvolved in the children's lives. Michelle, for example, placed at a predominantly low income, high minority population school, was worried about a boy in her class who was having a great deal of difficulty staying on task and completing his work. Michelle reported that her cooperating teacher helped him as much as possible at school, but acknowledged that the teacher "can't do anything to help him at home and no one there seems to care. I feel horrible! I want to do something to help this poor child."

Frustrated by her apparent lack of power, Michelle saw the child's parents as negligent villains and cast herself and her cooperating teacher as this child's saviors (Ayers, 1994). Sensing a clear boundary line drawn between home and school, Michelle felt that there was nothing she or her cooperating teacher could do to improve the child's situation. Partnership and communication with the boy's parents appeared to be out of the question: in her view, no one at his home "seems to care."

In her classic study of parent-teacher relations, Lightfoot (1977, p. 400) explains:

> One of the predominant myths about black parents and poor parents who surround inner-city schools is that they (1) do not care about the education of their children, (2) are passive and unresponsive to attempts by teachers and administrators to get them involved, and (3) are ignorant and naive about the cognitive and social needs of their children.

Just as Lightfoot's work suggests, I found these particular concerns and attitudes frequently expressed by those preservice teachers, like Michelle, whose placements were in schools enrolling high numbers of children of color living in poverty. For example, Maria was placed in a first grade classroom at Green Oaks, a public school whose student population comprises entirely African American and Hispanic children, most of whom receive free or reduced-price lunch. In an early ejournal entry, Maria contemplated the challenges she faced regarding classroom management, and wrote:

> I feel Green Oaks students require a firm hand because they come from dysfunctional homes where there is no element of structured discipline. In many instances these children are literally on their own and used to doing what they want to do.

In his assessment of the relationship between the colonizer and the colonized, Albert Memmi (1965) found that those in power tended to view those less-powerful not as individuals but rather as one lumpen mass characterized simply by their status as "other." Memmi referred to this as "the mark of the plural" (Memmi, 1965, p. 85). Like the colonizer-colonized context, schools are settings where issues of power and privilege are institutionalized and enacted (Foucault, 1977a, 1977b, 1978, 1982; Gore, 1993; McLaren, 1994); Maria's assessment of her students' family lives seems to bear the mark of the plural. Maria asserted that all of the students at her school site need a firm hand, apparently because of the uniformly "dysfunctional" homes and undisciplined upbringings that she assumed to be an inevitable by-product of life in low SES families of color.

As Lightfoot wrote, many teachers "have developed strong negative images of parents which justify their exclusion from the schooling process without actually knowing them" (Lightfoot, 1977, p. 400). Maria was not a parent herself, and Maria had never met the parents of any of her pupils. Unconcerned with the families' funds of knowledge or the nuances of cross-cultural communication, Maria simply believed that the children's parents were not doing their job properly. As a caring teacher, Maria felt that she had no choice but to take on the responsibility for providing the children with the discipline and structure necessary to be successful in school. Maria's emerging conception of the boundaries of a teacher's responsibility allowed her to feel comfortable offering a blanket indictment of the child-rearing strategies practiced by her students' families.

Many of Maria's classmates were placed in high SES schools enrolling primarily Anglo children. In these particular schools, the parent community tended to be highly visible and involved with their children's education; underinvolvement and lack of structured discipline in the home were rarely a concern of the preservice teachers placed in those schools. However, those preservice teachers could still be dissatisfied with their pupils' parents' ability to do their job properly. For example, Kay felt that the parents of one of her students were being too hard on him. She wrote:

> Bob's parents expect more out of him than he is capable [of producing]. His father is a brain surgeon — brilliant — and cannot accept that Bob may not be on as high an academic level . . . Over spring break, Bob's father made him bring home his math book so that they could drill fraction problems while Bob had some "free time." This is exactly the WRONG kind of motivation Bob needs.

As in the "bad parent" scenarios spun by Maria and Michelle, Kay told a story in which her efforts to do right by a child were thwarted by parental inadequacies or disinterest. Kay believed she knew the appropriate motivational techniques to use with Bob, and felt frustrated by the decisions Bob's father was making on his son's behalf. It appears that in Kay's growing understanding of the ways that caring manifests itself in a teacher's work, a caring teacher knows the children in her class better than their own parents do.

Like Kay, many of the students appeared to assume that "teacher knows best." In fact, some of my preservice teachers began to believe that they cared for and understood the children better than anyone else could. The following quotes from Mary's and Maria's ejournals illustrate this phenomenon well:

> I hope I have touched their lives to the point that if they should ever feel unloved or alone, they will know that I love them and as long as they have a thought of me, they will never be alone. Once more, I can only hope this will fill them with a sense of happiness and a drive to continue for success! (Mary)

> I know I care for students, even rotten ones, when I can put their faults to the side and dig deep for one inkling of good spirit . . . . Although it is more challenging, it is also useful to the child. I keep in mind that others might not care, so it is left up to me to make a difference during the time they are under my wings. (Maria)

This "teacher knows best" stance often surfaced as the students questioned the motivations, feelings, and intent of their children's parents. This was particularly apparent when children were experiencing difficulties at school. After learning that one of his pupils would be receiving medication for a behavioral disorder, Mark wondered:

> Are [his parents] really providing him the best care he deserves? I believe if they truly care for this child they should have exhausted all other options before placing him on medication.

As a student teaching intern, Mark was not privy to conversations about the range of options these parents had pursued, nor was he aware of the emotional energy the parents had invested in their decision to medicate their child. Mark, indignant, simply assumed that the parents did not "truly care" for their son.

Similarly, when Ariel learned that one of the children in her class was unexpectedly withdrawn from the school and would not be returning, she felt a great deal of anger and indignation:

> Why couldn't she have come just one more day to say good-bye? Why couldn't her family wait until the semester end or even until spring break? How come Jessica couldn't say good-bye to her friends?

Though she had no knowledge of the circumstances surrounding the student's withdrawal, Ariel certainly had a clear sense of what a caring family's priorities would have been in the situation; this family fell short of those expectations.

Knowles & Holt-Reynolds (1991) point out that "preservice teachers sometimes use alternate and potentially dysfunctional rationales for interpreting classroom events and making instructional decisions" (Knowles & Holt-Reynolds, 1991, p. 88). As they struggled to make meaning out of what they were witnessing and experiencing in their field placement classrooms, many of the preservice teachers developed explanations that were adversarial and disrespectful toward their pupils' parents. Although I was troubled by the idealistic, simplistic, and essentialist beliefs about the relationship of caring and teaching that my preservice teachers brought with them to their field placements, I found their new-found understandings — or, in the tactful words of Knowles & Holt-Reynolds, their "alternate and potentially dysfunctional rationales" — to be significantly more problematic. In the case of the dilemmas about parent-teacher-child relationships, the students' stance reflected a move toward short-sighted arrogance rather than toward the open-hearted commitment to partnership expected of responsible professionals. So much for those gentle smiles and warm hugs.

It must be noted that the students' beliefs about the relationships between teaching and caring did not change dramatically over the course of this study: the disequilibrium caused by their first field placements was followed by a slowly-growing awareness of the need for new understandings and conceptions, and a gradual stretching toward reconceptualized perspectives, both good and bad. Furthermore, because the students were at the very beginning stages of their professional lives, the images, ideas, beliefs, and understandings they held at the end of this study and documented in this chapter are unlikely to be stable: this slow process of growth and change will continue throughout these students' teaching careers. In other words, I am not willing to write these students off.

However, I am also not willing to ignore what happened. Their development of such negative, disturbing opinions about parents warrants close examination. Was this a case of the impact of university course work being "washed out" by field experience (Zeichner & Tabachnick, 1981)? Perhaps the students were exposed to negative influences from cooperating teachers or from other classroom or institutional factors (Zeichner & Grant, 1991)? Or might there be other external sources for the degeneration of their attitudes (Zeichner, 1980)?

Research has documented field placement as a stressful experience for preservice teachers (Jelinek, 1986; MacDonald, 1993). I can see a range of potentially stressful factors in my students' experience that might have led to poor decision-making and lapses in judgment. For example, the literature indicates that undergraduate preservice teachers have a wide range of fears and concerns about working with their students' parents (Foster & Loven, 1992), indeed, most preservice teachers are poorly prepared for this particular aspect of a classroom teacher's professional responsibility (Greenwood & Hickman, 1991).

During the course of this study, my preservice teachers had their first opportunities to play the role of professional in interactions with parents, and it is likely that they were fearful participants in these interactions. Although generally known for his work as a Jedi master and not as a teacher educator, Yoda made a comment in the movie *Star Wars Episode I: The Phantom Menace* that succinctly summarizes my students' experience with their children's parents: "fear leads to anger, anger leads to hate, hate leads to suffering" (Lucas, 1999). Because my students probably felt somewhat afraid of interacting with the parents, they developed negative attitudes and high levels of frustration and animosity.

Other potentially stressful factors were related to the students' social and cultural identities in contrast to those of their students. Most of my students came from white, middle-class families firmly rooted in mainstream U.S. culture, and many were placed at schools in low-income neighborhoods that served communities of color. When white preservice teachers do field placements in low-income schools with large populations of minority students, they are often faced with a range of challenges. For example, McIntyre's students had anxieties about their ability to teach effectively in such settings and about how they would be perceived by the children (McIntyre, 1997). It seems, then, that those students who were operating beyond the borders of their own cultural contexts for the first time in their lives had additional sources of stress to contend with in their field placements.

Finally, I believe that the students' gentle smiles and warms hugs view of caring might have been a significant factor in their exhaustion, stress and the resultant negativity. At the outset of the study, the students' beliefs about caring were idealistic and simplistic: recall Ariel writing that "a caring teacher is one who is truly devoted to improving and educating fellow members of the human race." Most believed, like Mary, that they could "care for all children for the special individuals they are and for what they have to share with the world" and, like Mark, that they would "be available for the child in any capacity and should never turn a deaf ear on a child's problem or concern."

For my students, caring was a personality trait, a disposition, a set of behaviors. Maria's definition captures this view well: "a caring teacher was one who is kind, loving, patient and one who never raises his/her voice at the students." Perhaps the burden of living up to this impossibly unrealistic expectation for personal devotion—only Mary Poppins could be this perfect!—was more than my preservice teachers could bear and contributed to their difficulties.

The research literature supports this supposition. Hargreaves & Tucker (1991) contend that "a narrow or exclusive orientation to care as personal care can actually lead to less care rather than more" (Hargreaves & Tucker, 1991, p. 497). Weinstein (1998) points out that preservice teachers who see caring "solely in terms of warmth and affection" (Weinstein, 1998, p. 155) might not see the connections between caring and academic expectations, or might be unwilling to exert the authority necessary to maintain a productive learning environment. It seems probable that the students' gentle smiles and warm hugs view of caring made their teaching experiences more difficult.

Had my students rooted their teaching in a vision of caring as a moral and intellectual relation, it is likely that they would have been able to build on the pedagogical power of caring in their work with children, create a powerful professional stance for themselves, and avoid some of the disastrous challenges they encountered. Why didn't this happen? I explore this question in chapter 6.

SECTION III

TEACHING ABOUT
CARING TEACHING:
A TEACHER EDUCATOR'S
PERSPECTIVES AND REFLECTIONS

Chapter 6

Confronting Failures in Caring

It would seem at first glance that the preservice teachers involved in this study were very well supported by the structure of our university's highly regarded teacher education program. The students were in daily contact with professors during the semester in which this study took place: they were enrolled in three methods courses, a course in learning and development, and the classroom organization and management course in which this study was embedded, and logged at least 20 hours of field experience each week. The students had weekly ejournal dialogue exchanges with me, their professor, and they had regular one-on-one meetings with Vickie, their fieldwork supervisor.

However, despite this apparent support, many of the students developed attitudes and beliefs about "caring" teaching—specifically, adversarial attitudes toward parents and negative perceptions of parents of color living in poverty—that were terribly disturbing. This left me wondering what could have been done differently.

I have a range of answers. Some are general, institutional, and easy to discuss. Others are personal and much more challenging to address.

Institutional solutions

My initial round of considerations revealed room for improvement both in the university's teacher education program and in the course I teach; the suggestions I offer here will also be useful to teacher educators in other elementary education teacher education programs.

Working to ensure that all of the preservice teachers' course instructors hold common images of the kinds of caring teachers we are hoping to prepare in our program and also share a commitment to working together to achieve those goals would be important first steps in improving the program (Rogers & Webb, 1991). According to the literature, field placement can be a time of great instability (Cole & Knowles, 1993; Zeichner & Tabachnick, 1981). The students might be less vulnerable at this tenuous time in their professional lives if their coursework experience at the university sent uniform messages about caring, teaching, and the moral and intellectual responsibility of teachers. Increasing communication and collaboration among course instructors would be another way to provide our preservice teachers with images of caring teaching that are clear, consistent, and positive.

Cooperating teachers' influence on preservice teachers' images and understandings of teaching must not be underestimated (Borko & Mayfield, 1995; Graham, 1999; Nettle, 1998). As a result, teacher educators and other university staff involved in the field placement process must strive to establish relationships with cooperating teachers and other significant school personnel who embody the values and ideals communicated by the university coursework and who model the caring practices and attitudes we hope our students to acquire. Although this might sound like a statement of the obvious, all too often high quality classroom placements can be difficult to come by and compromises are made at the expense of our preservice teachers' growth and development.

The findings in this study suggest it is unwise to assume preservice teachers' ideas about the relationship between caring and teaching will become richer, more thoughtful, and more sophisticated as a natural course of events during their field placement period. In order to ensure preservice teachers' incoming preconceptions, beliefs, and assumptions about caring are replaced by a range of more sophisticated understandings, this issue must be confronted head-on and addressed directly. This could take place within a practicum class linked to the students' field placements, such as the classroom organization and management course that I teach. In a course designed around the results of this study, students would engage in a process of critical self-examination, working to identify their preconceptions, beliefs, and assumptions about the relationship of caring and teaching. Incorporating the teacher education literature documenting the stability of preservice teachers' beliefs (Kagan, 1992) and the findings of this study with an explicit discussion exploring the students' existing understandings of caring is one way to lead students to a greater meta-awareness of the processes of becoming a caring teacher.

This approach could be enhanced by including a critical media literacy component (Freedman, 1999). An examination of representations of teachers in popular culture would make explicit the socio-cultural scripts being enacted in classrooms, making the "hegemony of nice" opaque and visible to preservice teachers. Exploring images of teachers and teaching in children's books is another way to make explicit the beliefs and assumptions commonly held about, and held by, elementary teachers (Joseph & Burnaford, 1994).

Engaging students with texts and course materials that directly challenge their pat and comfortable notions of caring is another possible approach. Reading works directly related to caring in classrooms that explore the relationship between caring and power (Noblit, 1993) or that force students to confront the issues of race, culture, and colonization inherent in caring (Delpit, 1988; Eaker-Rich & Van Galen, 1996) would stimulate conversation and require that students rethink their personal stance on care in relation to work with children.

Yet another possibility would be to require preservice elementary teachers to interview practicing teachers about the role of caring in their daily work. In addition to questioning "typical" teachers working in the elementary grades, interviewing secondary school teachers and/or male teachers at any grade level might help students to unpack and explore the ways that caring, gender, and work with younger children have been merged.

Next, students should have structured opportunities to engage in conversations about the ways in which those strongly held beliefs about the relationships between caring and teaching are being and will be challenged and changed over the course of the semester's field placement experiences. Explicit discussions about the new beliefs and assumptions students have and will continue to develop would provide useful opportunities for course instructors to offer the guidance and support needed to ensure that the new beliefs about caring are carefully considered and oriented toward the development of attitudes and practices that will prepare the students for success as caring teachers.

These discussions could be enhanced by reading selected articles, such as Cole & Knowles's "Shattered Images: Understanding Expectations and Realities of Field Experiences" (Cole & Knowles, 1993) that vividly depict the personal, emotional, and intellectual tumult that are an inevitable part of teaching field placements. In addition, recent graduates from our program who are employed in local schools settings could also be tapped as a source of support and information for our preservice teachers. Real world stories of preconceptions challenged and beliefs changed coming directly from practicing teachers who were in our students' shoes only months before are likely to have a different effect than the same information coming from a university professor or a graduate student field supervisor.

Because caring is often taken for granted and underdiscussed within teacher education, students are able to labor under all kinds of mistaken impressions about what it takes and what it means to teach with care. I contend that, rather than assuming that we all know caring when we see it (Rogers & Webb, 1991), we need to develop an orientation toward teacher education in which students' pre-existing beliefs about caring and teaching are called into question, scrutinized critically, and then thoughtfully re-integrated into their evolving practices.

Personal failures

I sat down to read the students' ejournal entries at the close of the first week of the data collection period of the study. My preservice teachers were going to share with me some of their initial thoughts about being a caring teacher. I could hardly wait as I logged on to my email account. I began to read:

> A caring teacher is an individual who cares about students in many special ways. (Thuy)

> One of my initial reasons for wanting to become a teacher is because I care so much about children. I absolutely love them! (Kay)

> A caring teacher is one who is truly devoted to improving and educating fellow members of the human race. (Ariel)

> Caring is a characteristic that I think all students who want to be teachers possess. (Leigh)

> A caring teacher means different things to different people. . . . A caring teacher . . . has to have love, love, and more love for children. (Roberta)

> My goal is to care for all children for the special individuals they are and for what they have to share with the world. (Mary)

Honestly, although I expected to read about gentle smiles and warm hugs, I was surprised by the tenor and the stance expressed in many of these journal entries. They were disturbingly reminiscent of the empty platitudes proffered by contestants in televised beauty pageants.

As the study progressed, I was somewhat irritated by the superficiality and romanticism that characterized the preservice teachers' incoming understandings of caring teaching. Well aware of the research highlighting the "central role played by pre-existing beliefs/images and prior experience" (Kagan, 1992, p. 140) in the development of teachers' practices and "the stability and inflexibility of prior beliefs and images" (Kagan, 1992, p. 140) during preservice teachers' training and induction, I feared that my preservice teachers were going to hold on to those simple perspectives and become those "gentle smiles and warm hugs" (Rogers, 1994, p. 33) caring teachers that troubled me so.

That fear was nothing compared to the horror I felt when I realized that as their field placement period progressed, some of my preservice teachers' understandings had somehow shifted from that simple, naive view of caring teaching to a conception of caring that led to hostile and adversarial beliefs about the parents of their students. I didn't much care for the gentle smiles and warm hugs, but this twisted vision of racist, classist teacherly caring was worse than I could have imagined.

How could this have happened? How could something so uncaring have occurred within the context of a caring study? What went wrong here?

After an embarrassingly long period of blaming my preservice teachers and blaming Nel Noddings and blaming Mother Teresa and Bob Geldof and Princess Diana and The Care Bears and anyone else I could think of who had ever been publicly linked with the word caring, and after a short period of general disgust with the whole endeavor of educational research, I began to question my own role in the creation and perpetuation of my students' beliefs and attitudes.

To do so more thoroughly, I brought the raw data from the study to the attention of Debra Freedman, a colleague involved in teacher education at my university but unconnected with this study, asking for her help in examining my own contributions to the formation and reinforcement of my students' troubling beliefs about caring teaching. Debra read and re-read all of the students' ejournal entries as an outsider to the study, marking and highlighting, posing questions, looking for inconsistencies, catching things Vickie and I had ignored, dropped, overlooked, let slide. Together she and I re-analyzed all of the study data from a new vantage point.

Our reinterpretation of the data from this study presented me with a troubling view of my role in this study. This story of my experience is important because it raises significant questions about the hegemonic nature of the dominant discourse of teacher education. This dominant discourse will pose challenges as we embark on the process of reclaiming caring in teacher education.

Playing the game of school

My tidy narratives of caring were first called into question as Debra and I re-read the anonymous formative course evaluations written toward the middle of the semester-long study. Several students expressed resistance to and exasperation with my focus on caring. For example, in response to a request to discuss the usefulness of the dialogue ejournals, students wrote comments along the lines of these:

> Need to have more freedom of choice. Having the topic "caring" already chosen for us limits us from getting other information we may desire.

> It's nice to have the opportunity to carry on a one-on-one dialogue with you, but I feel kind of restricted if I have to talk about caring in an overt way.

In addition, students found the emphasis on caring to be repetitive and even unpleasant. One student stated that rather than being helpful, the ejournal dialogues were "stress-inducing: 'What more can I say about caring?'"
This sentiment was echoed by another student who wrote:

> What a pain! I don't like them because I don't always have something to write about [caring].

Although I had blithely dismissed the students' complaints at the time—the students were not obligated to write about caring; that had been made clear to them time and time again—when we revisited the study data looking for fresh insights into the situation, the realization that caring was problematic for these preservice teachers was a site of paradox and tension for me. I had thought that they had agreed with my perspectives on the importance of caring in teaching-learning relationships and in classroom contexts.

Did they agree? Or had I been hoodwinked? Could I ever know? The preservice teachers in this study knew the golden rule of the game of school (Fried, 1995): good students do what their teachers ask of them. Realizing this gave me new insight into the preservice teachers' Miss America-isms that I'd found so unappealing and revealed one possible explanation for their banality: those comments are hollow and shallow because they were written to meet a requirement rather than to express genuine emotion. I had asked the students to write journal entries focused on caring, so the preservice teachers were doing their best to give me what I seemed to want.

As I re-read the dialogue journal entries again and again, it became clear that my emphasis on caring forced the students to wedge their thoughts and experiences into the invisible framework I had constructed for them. Suddenly ejournal entries that I had read countless times, interpreted, and come to understand looked different.

In chapter 4, I shared a quote from Rosita's ejournal. I had asked the students to consider the role of caring in their cooperating teachers' practices. Rosita wrote:

> The environment was cluttered and there were posters that were falling down, I took this to be some form of caring. . . . The relationship between teacher and student was interesting. I never saw her hug a child, or say good morning. She put children in time out quite often. . . . I have looked very hard for the caring relationship between teacher and student, it must be what they call tough love. I know she cares for her students, I need to figure it out for myself.

I had understood this quote as an example of the students' tendency to see caring and teaching as inextricably intertwined. I held Rosita up as an example: even when a cooperating teachers' practices were clearly uncaring, the preservice teachers still worked to see them as caring. Now I see that Rosita was drawing these conclusions not because she was shortsighted about caring, but because she had to write a journal entry about caring and did the best she could given that she had been placed in a cluttered and shabby classroom environment with a cooperating teacher exhibiting rude behavior toward students[1].

Another example, also from chapter 4. Like Rosita, Maria was looking for caring teaching. She wrote in her weekly ejournal entry:

> All week long as I pondered over this journal, I asked myself, "How can I write an [entry] on caring?" Then as I was observing Ms. Ziffle, I thought of this question and then asked myself, "Is Ms. Ziffle a caring teacher?" At first, I told myself "no" but then as I thought about what "caring" exactly meant, I told myself "Yes, she is a caring teacher." At this point, I asked myself "Why is she a caring teacher?" and I came up with the following reasons. . . .
>
> Before observing Ms. Ziffle, I thought a caring teacher was one who is kind, loving, patient and one who never raises his/her voice at the students. Now, I am sure this type of teacher exists and is successful in educating his/her students, but at a school like Green Oaks,[2] this type of teacher would not be in control of his/her class. . . .
>
> I feel Ms. Ziffle recognizes this dilemma and has more respect for her children than to place them in this type of situation. That is why I feel her combination of instilling strict discipline and having a special love towards them at the same time makes her a caring teacher. My understanding of a caring teacher is now broader.

Maria wracked her brain to stretch her definition of caring to encompass Ms. Ziffle's practices. It took her all week to develop an understanding of the "special love" that her cooperating teacher feels for the children, a love that does not involve kindness, loving patience, or a gentle voice, just so she could complete her assignment.

Because I asked my preservice teachers to look for caring, they felt compelled to find some and, as a result, ended up calling all kinds of questionable and potentially harmful practices "caring."

---

[1]Rosita's placement was changed the following week.

[2]As I mentioned in chapter 5, Green Oaks is a low-performing elementary school with a student population comprising low-income African American and Hispanic American children.

Though it clearly caused some cognitive dissonance for the student teachers—particularly the two quoted here—no one was willing to question or to interrogate either my assumptions or their cooperating teachers' practices. They just wanted to do their ejournal assignment and get on with their lives.

As I re-read the students' ejournals, I also saw that my single-minded devotion to caring may also have sent the message that caring was a magic panacea that would make teaching easy and smooth. Roberta wrote:

> How do you keep on giving unconditional love when you are at the end of your rope?. . . . I just do not understand how you keep going when you are frustrated and tired. Hopefully, with our study of "caring" I will discover some answers.

As I mentioned in chapter 4, Roberta had a life crisis later in the semester. She described her feelings in her journal:

> I thought that I was not cut out to be a teacher. I thought that I did not have enough of the qualities to be a good teacher. . . . As you might expect, my parents freaked out. . . . I have always wanted to be a teacher as long as I can remember. . . . Just recently I have doubted everything in myself and really struggled to find what it takes to teach, to be a really good teacher.

I never got a sense of what precipitated this particular crisis. Did Roberta feel that she didn't care enough? That she couldn't possibly care enough to be successful? That she didn't have the requisite caring personality? Did I cause the crisis—did I hold up caring as some ideal, an impossible dream, and since perfection is not attainable, Roberta felt like a failure?

I had set the expectation that caring would be a focus of the course and of classroom teaching; the students dutifully responded by trusting me and working hard to function within my guidelines. I myself was so deeply entrenched in that worldview that it had become invisible to me; I was unaware that my focus on caring was oppressive and limiting for the students.

Caring became a regime of truth, the only correct way of looking at, responding to, and participating in classroom life.

A right way to care?

I explicitly root my working understandings of caring in the philosophies of Nel Noddings (1984). To recap, in Noddings's description, caring involves three actions on the part of the caregiver: receptivity, engrossment, and motivational displacement. In a caring encounter, the one-caring is expected to put aside her own concerns and to receive the cared-for fully, becoming engrossed in the cared-for's perceptions and goals. To be one-caring, according to Noddings's view, one must focus intensely on the needs and desires of those for whom you are caring.

However, I see that I found it difficult to operationalize these Noddings-informed beliefs in this caring study. In re-reading the students' ejournals, it seemed that rather than engaging in motivational displacement, putting aside my own concerns and desires and taking on those of my cared-fors, I generally held my ground and worked to bring the students to see situations from my point of view.

A journal exchange between one of the preservice teachers and me about classroom management illustrates this well. Thuy, the student, described her own style of caring teaching in her journal:

> I believe the students in Mrs. Saks's class know that I truly care about them through the following descriptions. First I am always excited and care very much to be at the school to help them. Every morning that I am here, I check their homework for correct completion. When the assignment is properly done, they receive stickers for their work. If the child turns in an incomplete assignment, I call the kid up and demonstrate an example correctly. Then the child is to finish the work at his or her desk. Once the child completes the assignment, a sticker is given to him or her. The reward is to let them know I care about their work and to encourage them to succeed. . . .

My response to Thuy challenges her beliefs in what appears to be an appropriate, teacherly way:

> You surely came across as a strong supporter of rewards/stickers, behavior charts and the like. In light of Thursday's class activities and discussions about Alfie Kohn's work, how are you feeling now?
>
> Can you write me a rationale explaining why you want to use these strategies in your classroom? How would you defend your beliefs if Alfie Kohn, or someone like him, challenged you to a debate?

However, in my analytic notes to myself, I was much less generous with Thuy. I wrote:

> Hello? What is up with Thuy? She is so very secure and confident in her understandings of how to teach and what good teaching is . . . and she is so off base! It seems that nothing we have said in class is in any way impacting her thinking about her practices. How can we problematize things for her, get her to REALLY think and REALLY reflect?

It seems that I saw my role as providing the students with the information they would need to become "good teachers." This was based, of course, on my own sense of what it means to be a good teacher. When Thuy clearly wanted to use practices that I disapproved of, I was unwilling to support or celebrate Thuy's successes—I just kept on trying to change what Thuy believed. My own journal entry, in which I wonder how I can get Thuy to "REALLY think and REALLY reflect" reveals that I felt Thuy was neither thinking nor reflecting simply because Thuy's thoughts and reflections were not in line with my own.

In the journal excerpt quoted above, Thuy says point-blank that these classroom strategies are a demonstration of her care for the children in her class. So, in my blanket condemnation of Thuy's preferred teaching practices, I was also disallowing Thuy's form of caring. To me, then, Thuy's behaviorist mode of rewarding the kids was not only bad teaching, it was also bad caring.

Is there a right way to care? It seems that I might have believed so: I certainly praised other student teachers for their relational work with their children. The preservice teachers who received the warmest responses from me were those whose practices and beliefs lined up most closely with my own.

I began this data re-analysis process with Debra because I was disappointed in my students. After our re-analysis and re-interpretation of the study data, I was disappointed in myself, disappointed by the choices I had made in my interactions with the students.

Looking at it now, though, I see things differently. The problem is bigger than I suspected: my students and I are all trapped in a pervasive grand narrative of teacher education.

Gore, drawing on Foucault, argues that all social institutions create and maintain regimes of truth about how one should think, act, and feel (Gore, 1993). Operating through the hegemony of norms, these regimes of truth shape the ways in which one identifies and acts (Best & Kellner, 1991), thus maintaining a certain status quo. Teacher education has its own set of hegemonic practices and beliefs that have become a regime of truth, invisibly influencing and dominating the field.

Although my course may have been designed with a focus on caring, the course itself was embedded within a much larger and more powerful teacher education juggernaut fueled by the dominant discourses of teacher education. This study took place within an established teacher education program at a large, well-regarded research university in the United States; approximately 300 elementary teachers are graduated from our program each year.

Like a fish unaware of the water around her, I designed this study without consideration of the values and assumptions secretly underlying my course and my research plan. The belief that preservice teacher reflection leads to enhanced practice, the implicit understanding that dialogue with professors is beneficial to students, and the assumption that professors have the right to require certain kinds of writing and topics, to judge students, and to make students into the "right" kind of teacher are examples of some of the truths that operate within teacher education's hegemony of norms and lurk within my syllabus and my caring study.

Do I hold these assumptions to be true? More importantly, do these assumptions make sense within a care-centered approach to teacher education? Do they allow me to meet my preservice teachers as one-caring, to act with special regard for each student in a non-rulebound way (Noddings, 1984, p. 24)?

Looking at the findings of my study, I see that the approach to teacher education which emerges from the dominant discourse, the approach within which I worked in this study, did not allow my preservice teachers to develop the kind of attitudes and beliefs about caring that would prepare them to take advantage of the pedagogical power of caring. Instead, this approach to teacher education allowed the preservice teachers to play the game of school, to give me what I appeared to want, to develop racist and classist ideas about children and families, and to adopt adversarial attitudes toward parents.

I accepted the practices, values and assumptions of mainstream teacher education without question, without examining whether or not those fit within a caring framework. This was a mistake.

Teacher education must help preservice teachers move beyond the gentle smiles and warm hugs view of teacherly caring toward an understanding of caring as a moral and intellectual relation. My findings in this study suggest that this will not be possible working within the current mainstream discourse of teacher education.

I suspect that the solutions that I offered at the start of this chapter are doomed to fail. Although they look like improvements, they operate within the rules, norms, and assumptions of the existing systems of teacher education that we have in place. The task now, then, is to envision a new form of teacher education that will allow us to engage in care-centered teacher education and to prepare teachers to claim caring as a meaningful professional stance and to build on the pedagogical power of caring in their work with children.

Chapter 7

Toward a Vision of
Caring Teacher Education:
The Cornerstones of Caring Model

In the past decade there has been a great deal of interest in incorporating caring into teacher education. For example, there are a number of textbooks that are specifically aimed at helping preservice teachers develop care-centered practice that have been published for use in teacher education courses. A glance at the shelf in my office where I keep the texts that are sent to me to preview for use in the Classroom Organization and Management class that formed the heart of this study reveals a number that have care or love mentioned explicitly in the title: *Teaching Children to Care* (Charney, 1992); *Among Friends: Classrooms Where Caring and Learning Prevail* (Dalton & Watson, 1997); *Curriculum of Love* (Daleo, 1996); and *The Caring Teacher's Guide to Discipline* (Gootman, 1997). There are more — *Life in a Crowded Place* (Peterson, 1992), *Teaching with Heart* (Diero, 1996), *Because We Can Change The World* (Sapon-Shevin, 1999), for example — that do not mention caring explicitly but that are also rooted firmly in an ethic of care.

I imagine that there are many professors in many college and university teacher education programs using these texts with the best intentions and with goals well aligned with mine. However, making the decision to use one of these textbooks — even the most innovative and radical of them — is making a decision to work squarely within the dominant discourse and structures of mainstream teacher education. My experience with the preservice teachers in this study suggests that working within the dominant discourse makes the establishment of truly care-centered teacher education practice extremely difficult, if not impossible.

Barbara Arnstine (1990) agrees with my assessment. She offers a scathing critique of existing teacher education practices, arguing that the fundamental values, assumptions, and goals of teacher education programs make it virtually impossible to develop caring teachers within them. She writes:

> The activities of students in a teacher preparation program are remarkably similar in character to those of their pupils in the public schools. Teacher preparation programs are designed to deliver a predetermined curriculum that fulfills credential requirements in a short period of time. They use a system of competitive grading that reassures the rest of the campus that teacher education is academically respectable. Thus, prospective teachers are encouraged to obey authority and to work alone and independently. When school experiences consistently call for obedience and competition, even the most obvious possibilities for acting in a rational and caring way go unrecognized (Arnstine, 1990, pp. 241-2).

If we want to prepare teachers who will be able to draw upon a moral and intellectual relation view of caring to build a strong foundation for their professional practices and to take advantage of the pedagogical power of caring in their work with students, we must design teacher education programs specifically focused toward those ends.

In virtually all of the available literature on caring and teacher education, caring has been simply added on to the existing program. To use Larry Cuban's terminology, these care-centered innovations have been examples of "first-order changes," reform efforts in which people "try to make what already exists more efficient and more effective without disturbing the basic organizational features" of the program (Cuban, 1988, p. 342).

For example, Rosiek (1994) suggests using teacher narratives as a way to create a care-centered form of teacher education. While I agree with his argument that "narratives are much better suited to capturing the relational complexity of a situation than are scientific principles or analytic essays" (Rosiek, 1994, p. 23), I think that an "add narratives and stir" approach to creating care-centered teacher education is unlikely to have the broad impact that he would like. Swick (1999) advocates the use of service learning to strengthen preservice teachers' caring perspectives. However, like Rosiek, Swick situates his care-centered pedagogical strategy within existing teacher education structures. Instead of this type of additive, incremental change, I believe teacher education needs care-centered innovations that represent "second order changes" (Cuban, 1988, p. 342). Cuban describes reforms of this type: "Second-order changes seek to alter the fundamental ways in which organizations are put together. They reflect major dissatisfactions with present arrangements. Second-order changes introduce new goals, structures, and roles that transform familiar ways of doing things into new ways of solving persistent problems" (Cuban, 1988, p. 342).

Henderson (1988) effected care-centered second-order changes in a preservice teacher education seminar, demonstrating that such a feat is indeed possible. Drawing on Noddings's (1984) ideas, he designed the seminar around his own interpretation of the ethic of care's key pedagogical facets. First, he felt students would need to experience themselves as the initiators of their own professional growth, and second, he believed that there would have to be a great deal of focus on the students as individuals. Henderson's two innovations emerged directly from Noddings's theories: in the article describing this course development experience he supports both of those points with direct quotations from Noddings's work.

Henderson also reconceptualized his own pedagogical practices, discarding his usual operating procedures and adopting strategies and perspectives rooted in Noddings's work. He stated:

> To be consistent, I realized that my own instruction would need to be grounded in an ethic of caring. I would need to be committed to an open-ended dialogue with each student and to practicing the art of "confirming" (Noddings, 1984) their inquiries into meaningful professional growth. In succinct terms, though I had devised a rational plan of action, the students' growth needs, not the plan, would be my central concern. (Henderson, 1988, p. 91)

What I find most powerful about Henderson's curriculum reform effort is the way in which he grounded his pedagogical actions in a theoretical foundation, and then used that foundation to support his decisions throughout the course. No gentle smiles and warm hugs from Henderson; he understood Noddings's work and offered his students an educational experience rooted in a view of caring as a moral and intellectual relation.

I have followed in Henderson's footsteps, engaging in a process of theory-driven second-order change to envision a radically different form of care-centered teacher education. In this chapter I outline my vision, called the Cornerstones of Caring (CoC) model, which draws upon the work of Nel Noddings (1984), Robert Sternberg (1988a, 1988b), Robert Fried (1995) and others to create a teacher education program centered in a view of caring as a moral and intellectual relation, an approach that will position caring as a crucial factor in the teaching-learning process and a powerful intellectual stance for teachers.

Nel Noddings and teacher education

Building on her powerfully influential work on caring and believing that caring is "a type of relationship that can be promoted by sound practices in teacher education and supervision" (Noddings, 1999, p. 205), Nel Noddings developed a theoretical model for care-centered teacher education (Noddings, 1986). The heart of this model is a fundamental, second-order change from the typical, business-as-usual practices in teacher education programs. Noddings argues that rather than talking of teacher education in terms of "content, selection of students, exit tests, and credentials" (Noddings, 1986, p. 505), we must think of teacher education in terms of modeling, dialogue, practice, and confirmation.

Modeling demands that we treat our preservice teachers with the same attentive care that we wish them to bring to their interactions with children. Noddings states that the best way to ensure that our students will leave our teacher education programs and interact with children in a caring manner "is to demonstrate, in our own teaching, how teachers convey their caring" (Noddings, 1986, p. 503).

In Noddings's vision of teacher education, the pedagogical techniques and strategies presented to our students are not seen as skills to be mastered but rather as "material to be analyzed, discussed, critiqued, and considered" (Noddings, 1986, p. 504). She asserts that teacher educators must engage students in critical thinking and genuine dialogue about these matters of educational significance in order to prepare them to be critical thinkers and thoughtful decision-makers throughout their teaching careers.

Practice, the third component of Noddings's model, is a standard part of teacher preparation. However, Noddings's interpretation of the term is very specific: "Practice in teaching should be practice in caring. There is an attitude to be sustained and enhanced as well as a set of skills to be learned" (Noddings, 1986, p. 504). In order for this form of practice to occur, preservice teachers must be placed with carefully selected cooperating teachers who demonstrate fidelity to Noddings's understandings of caring teaching.

Noddings has called confirmation, the last component in her model of teacher education, "the loveliest of human functions" (Noddings, 1984, p. 196). Through our work in a teacher education program of this nature we confirm the ethical ideals toward which we strive, and we work to bring forth that best image in our students and in ourselves.

Although I agree with Noddings's assessments and I like all four dimensions of this model very much, I have concerns about adopting Noddings's model and positioning it at the heart of my reconceptualized vision of teacher education. My concerns relate to the key aspects of teacher education that her model overlooks.

First, Noddings's model lacks a strong focus on issues of community. The article in which she articulates her model of teacher education has several mentions of community, some of which are very powerful: for example, she states that we must approach our goal of creating caring moral persons "by living with those whom we teach in a caring community, through modeling, dialogue, practice, and confirmation" (Noddings, 1986, p. 502). However, when community is mentioned—in this teacher education article and throughout Noddings's work—it is rarely explored in depth.

This comes as no real surprise, given the nature of Noddings's understanding of caring. In Noddings's theory, caring is a relation centered in a one-on-one encounter between a one-caring and a cared-for. Larger groups can be formed through circles and chains of caring (Noddings, 1984), but the one-caring/cared-for inter-action is the heart of the theory. As a result, Noddings's understanding and discussion of caring teaching-learning epi-sodes within teacher education are generally located within inter-actions between the instructor and student. Noddings mentions that teacher educators should try to build caring communities (Noddings, 1986) but offers no strategies for community develop-ment within her model.

Rogers & Webb's (1991) work on care-centered teacher edu-cation acknowledges this shortcoming in Noddings's original vi-sion in its addition of a dimension—continuity—to Noddings's dimensions of modeling, dialogue, practice, and confirmation. Noting that caring relationships are formed through "continuous and sustained interpersonal contact with specific people" (Rogers & Webb, 1991, p. 179), they argue for a vision of teacher education that allows students to work with the same classmates, the same children, the same cooperating teachers, and the same faculty members for an extended period of time. They write: "It is unrealistic to expect student teachers to develop an understanding of the role of caring in classroom practice when fieldwork is a patchwork of disconnected classroom experiences" (Rogers & Webb, 1991, p. 179). Through their attention to continuity, Rogers & Webb offer preservice teachers the opportunity to be part of a caring community.

Membership in a caring community is important for pre-service teachers. Research has indicated that participation in co-hort groups (Goldstein, 2000), critical friendship groups (Achin-stein & Meyer, 1997; Meyer & Achinstein, 1998), and other forms of caring community (Kahne & Westheimer, 1992) is a powerful source of support, encouragement, and learning for preservice teachers. Also, the experience of being part of a caring community as a teacher education student prepares preservice teachers to offer that experience to the children they will teach in the future. In addition to the forms of pedagogical modeling advocated by Noddings (1986, p. 503) — "meticulous preparation, lively presentation, critical thinking, appreciative listening, constructive evaluation, genuine curiosity" — teacher education programs must also model classroom organization perspectives designed to enhance community.

My second concern about Noddings's vision of care-centered teacher education relates to the model's apparent lack of attention to issues of curriculum content. I say "apparent lack of attention" deliberately. In reality, Noddings holds subject matter and subject matter competence in high regard (Noddings, 1999). Noddings herself is a subject area specialist in mathematics and is a great advocate of teacher expertise in curricular content and academic knowledge. But these commitments are not readily visible in her model of teacher education, and that troubles me.

The boldness of statements such as "the student is infinitely more important than the subject" (Noddings, 1984, p. 20) and "Subject matter cannot carry itself. Relation, except in very rare cases, precedes any engagement with subject matter" (Noddings, 1992, p. 36) and the regularity with which she makes such statements suggest that Noddings elevates interpersonal relationships and denigrates mastery of academic knowledge. This plays right into the hands of those who believe that caring is all about gentle smiles and warm hugs, and works against my goals of reclaiming a moral and intellectual view of caring for teaching and teacher education.

Because of the pernicious, persistent, problematic nature of the "gentle smiles and warm hugs" view of caring, I feel uncomfortable with a model of care-centered teacher education that runs the risk of implying that caring teachers emphasize relationships and don't care about curriculum or learning. Any model of care-centered teaching that I would want to communicate to students must deal explicitly with the intellectual energy that caring teachers bring to the curriculum and to teaching, learning, and their professional decision-making.

Nel Noddings and I are in agreement about the importance of curriculum content in caring teaching, about the intellectual energy caring teachers bring to their work, and about the value of the moral and intellectual relation view of caring. However, unlike Noddings, I intend to address issues of curriculum and learning explicitly within my model of teacher education because I want to ensure that no one will be able to downplay the connections I wish to make between caring and intellectual life.

Noddings's work is excellent for understanding and supporting certain aspects of the process of teacher education. But taken by itself, it is insufficient. In conceptualizing the Cornerstones of Caring model, an approach to teacher education that is rooted in the moral and intellectual relation view of caring, I feel I must embed Noddings's work in a larger framework that will allow for an explicit commitment to the development of caring community and will also provide space for explicit consideration of care-centered habits of mind regarding curriculum and teaching practices. The Cornerstones of Caring model of teacher education is rooted in Noddings's theories about caring, and extends them in new directions.

Three cornerstones of caring teacher education

Psychologist Robert Sternberg (1988a; 1988b) has conceptualized a model of love that I believe holds great promise for the creation of a teacher education program rooted in the moral and intellectual relation view of caring. Although it was designed to depict the dimensions of adult-adult loving relationships, Sternberg's model of love is very flexible. With a few definitional modifications, I have used this model elsewhere with great success to delineate the contours of teacherly love (Goldstein, 1997), and I expect that Sternberg's model will be equally useful in offering a framework within which to consider the reconceptualization of teacher education.

As I mentioned briefly in chapter 5, Sternberg calls his model "the triangular theory of love" (1988a), and suggests that love can be understood in terms of three components—commitment, intimacy, and passion—that form the three sides of a triangle (see Figure 1).

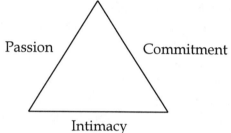

Figure 1

Commitment, in Sternberg's view, entails both the decision to love someone and the commitment to maintain that love; intimacy describes "the close, connected, and bonded feelings in loving relationships" (1988a, p. 120); and passion is "the drives that lead to romance, physical attraction, sexual consummation and the like" (1988a, p. 120).

I have used Sternberg's triangular model of love as a tool to guide the development of the Cornerstones of Caring approach to teacher education. Sternberg's three components of love—commitment, intimacy, and passion—defined in ways more relevant to our professional context form the cornerstones of this new vision. In the CoC model of teacher education, commitment is grounded in the fundamental responsibility of teacher educators and preservice teachers to enter into caring relationships with their students; intimacy is writ large and transformed into intimacy-in-community, leading to the creation of a community of learners sharing close personal connection; and passion is linked to efforts to ensure that our students see the connections between caring and the intellectual and curricular aspects of teaching children.

Before elaborating on the components of each cornerstone, I want to mention clearly that this triangular CoC model is meant to be a tool for organizing our thoughts and not a template for limiting or constricting our thinking. Although the model is neat and orderly, with its three distinct sections, teacher education is not. For the sake of clarity, I will address each cornerstone in turn. But that division is artificial and arbitrary to a certain extent and fails to capture the interconnectedness and complexity of the teacher education process.

In the following sections, I describe each cornerstone in detail and offer a general sense of how each cornerstone might be enacted within a teacher education program. I do not provide guidelines or checklists or indicators for each cornerstone, nor do I offer step-by-step recipes for enacting the CoC approach. The Cornerstones of Caring is an open-ended, flexible model that should be applied in many different ways in response to the varied needs and demands of specific teacher education programs in particular contexts; each time a teacher education program is organized around the Cornerstones of Caring a unique program will be created.

Cornerstone 1: Commitment

It is important at the outset to make a distinction between the commitment cornerstone of this model and the ways in which commitment is generally used when talking about teachers' caring practices (Acker, 1999; Hargreaves, 1994; Nias, 1989). For example, Hargreaves synthesizes a body of literature and writes about care, which is "interpreted as the interpersonal experience of human nurturance, connectedness, warmth, and love" (Hargreaves, 1994, p. 145), as a central, pervasive commitment widely shared by elementary teachers. This commitment to the gentle smiles and warm hugs view of caring is distinctly not what the commitment cornerstone of the CoC model represents.

Commitment as used in this model is also different from the commitment to caring teaching that most of our students bring to their teacher education programs. Exemplified by the ejournal entry posted by my student Roberta—"A caring teacher has to have love, love, and more love for children"—that form of commitment is more vague and general than the focused and specific commitment to meeting students as one-caring that is a driving force in the Cornerstones of Caring model of teacher education.

However, preservice teachers' incoming commitment to caring teaching is tremendously powerful and useful to care-centered teacher educators. The students' commitment to caring teaching, their prior assumptions and beliefs about teaching and learning, their strong desire to work with children, their previous experiences as students receiving care from teachers, and other aspects of their base of prior knowledge form the foundation upon which teacher educators can help students build a commitment to entering into caring relationships with their students.

The commitment cornerstone of CoC model emerges directly from Noddings's theories. Recall that in Noddings's view, caring is not a personality trait, but a relation. Noddings posits that every interaction provides us with the opportunity to enter into a caring relationship. As a result, each person stands at the same decision-making juncture many times each day and faces a choice: Will I approach this interaction as a caring encounter or will I not? Will I meet the other as one-caring? For Noddings, caring is a human obligation and the choice is clear: "One must meet the other in caring. From this requirement there is no escape for one who would be moral" (Noddings, 1984, p. 201).

Building on Noddings's ideas, then, caring teachers must make a commitment to meeting their students as one-caring, to approaching their interactions with their students as opportunities to engage in caring encounters. The central purpose of teacher education rooted in Noddings's ideas would be to develop in our preservice teachers the disposition to commit to meeting children as one-caring. Thus, commitment is a cornerstone of the CoC approach.

In order for preservice teachers to come to understand the importance of making a commitment to teaching with care, it will be necessary for teacher educators to do more than lecture about Noddings's theories: we must model those desired attitudes and behaviors. In other words, caring teacher educators must make a commitment to meeting their preservice teacher education students as one-caring, to approaching their interactions with their students as opportunities to engage in caring encounters. Earlier in this chapter, for example, I describe the way that Jim Henderson (1988) offers his preservice teacher education students an experience that demonstrates these principles.

Of course, Henderson's approach is not the only way to model caring teaching. Because "caring is a way of being in relation, not a set of specific behaviors" (Noddings, 1992, p. 17), there is a wide range of pedagogical strategies that would work well within the Cornerstones of Caring model of teacher education, including Noddings's suggestions of modeling, dialogue, practice and confirmation (Noddings, 1986).

There has been little scholarly attention focused on the nature of the caring relationships between university professors and their students or on the role of caring in teaching and learning in higher education (hooks, 1994; Thayer-Bacon & Bacon, 1996a, 1996b). However, I suspect that most teacher educators will acknowledge that the teacherly caring we feel for our preservice teacher education candidates is very much akin to the more widely-acknowledged teacherly caring we felt for our young students when we were classroom teachers (Goldstein, 1998b). Teacherly caring comes along with the pedagogical experience in the relational zone and has little to do with the age of the students or with the material being taught.

I would like to extend this parallel — drawing connections between the teaching-learning relationship of an elementary teacher and student and the teaching-learning relationship of a teacher educator and a preservice teacher — even further. I contend that the argument I made in chapter 2, that caring relationships are a prerequisite for intellectual growth, is equally true in teacher education contexts as in elementary school contexts. Grounding a teacher education program in the commitment to entering into caring relationships with students offers preservice teachers access to the cognitive growth that accompanies participation in caring teaching-learning interactions.

The Cornerstones of Caring model, rooted in a commitment to entering into caring teaching-learning relationships with preservice teachers, is a teacher education program that will create opportunities for preservice teachers' cognitive and professional growth.

The commitment cornerstone of the CoC model is coupled tightly to Nel Noddings's theories. As a result, modeling is a central facet of this cornerstone: teacher educators are modeling the commitment to caring we hope to see our preservice teachers enact with their young students. This emphasis on modeling has additional benefits. The teacher educators' conscious focus on modeling a commitment to caring is also preparing preservice teachers to extend to their future students the cognitive growth opportunities linked to caring teaching-learning relationships.

The commitment cornerstone demands a great deal of consistency, continuity, and affiliation to these ideas throughout a program aligned with the Cornerstones of Caring model. Teacher education programs host a range of nested and overlapping relational milieus of remarkable complexity, each a site rich with possibilities for caring teaching-learning interactions and intellectual growth for all involved: teacher education professors care for their preservice teacher education students, who in turn care for the children in their field placement classrooms; cooperating teachers care for both the preservice teacher education students and the young students in their classrooms, and so on. If any of the links in this chain of caring are weak, if any of the educators do not model a commitment to meeting their students as one-caring, the overall impact of the program will be compromised.

It might seem that the commitment cornerstone is an unrealistic expectation and an unattainable goal. Is it possible to maintain a commitment to meeting all students as one-caring? What happens when a teacher encounters a student that she just doesn't like? Noddings makes a distinction between natural caring and ethical caring that eases this pressure. Central to this distinction is the foundational belief that caring is not a feeling that one either has or does not have, but that caring is a relation that one chooses to enter into or not. Even if a teacher or teacher educator does not have spontaneous personal or social attraction toward a student, she is still capable of making a professional decision to meet that student in a caring manner.

Natural caring is "that relation in which we respond as one-caring out of love or natural inclination" (Noddings, 1984, p. 4-5). In cases of natural caring, "I must" is indistinguishable from "I want." Noddings (1984, p. 82-3) elaborates:

> When my infant cries in the night, I not only feel that I must do something, but I want to do something. Because I love this child, because I am bonded to him, I want to remove his pain as I would want to remove my own. The "I must" is not a dutiful imperative but one that accompanies the "I want." If I were tied to a chair, for example, and wanted desperately to get free, I might say as I struggled, "I must do something; I must get out of these bonds." But this "must" is not yet the moral or ethical "ought." It is a must born of desire.

Noddings asserts that natural caring is the human condition that we perceive as "good." As humans we strive toward that condition, "and it is that longing for caring—to be in that special relation—that provides the motivation for us to be moral" (Noddings, 1984, p. 4-5). This is an ethical ideal that undergirds Noddings's model.

There are many times, of course, when natural caring does not occur, times when the "I must" that accompanies the commitment to meet others as one-caring is not aligned with the "I want" rooted within the individual. Noddings acknowledges that there are many times when the "I must" whispers faintly and disappears and is then followed by the clamor of resistance (Noddings, 1984, pp. 82-3). In these cases, a second sentiment—"I ought"—is paired with "I must" to elicit a caring response. This "I ought" is a moral sentiment which compels the one-caring to enter a caring relation. The one-caring, in these cases, is motivated to respond not by natural caring feelings, but by her desire to be moral and her commitment to meet others with care: responding as one-caring is an act of volition, a conscious choice stemming from a moral aspiration. Noddings refers to this type of caring as ethical caring, since it is driven by an ethical ideal.

Though it requires an effort not needed in natural caring, ethical caring is not a diminished form of caring, nor is it less authentic than natural caring. Both natural and ethical caring require engrossment, receptivity, and motivational displacement on the part of the one-caring. Both natural caring and ethical caring begin with a sense of responsibility—"I must"—and with the commitment to meet others as one-caring. Both natural and ethical caring encounters move the one-caring and the cared-for closer to the ethical ideal, and both are sources of great joy and satisfaction. The difference between the two is linked to issues of motive: natural caring is driven by deep feelings for the cared-for; ethical caring is driven by the one-caring's desire to enhance her ethical ideal, her vision of herself as a moral person, or in the case of teaching, by the one-caring's professional commitment to teaching with these principles in mind.

A teacher who has made the choice to approach each interaction with her students as an opportunity to enter into a caring relation would be likely to experience both ethical and natural caring in those relationships. Let me illustrate with an example from my experience in Martha George's classroom in 1997. I had expected to like and to care for all of the students in Martha's class and was unhappy to find that was impossible.

In some cases—Andy, for example—time and perseverance led to a solution. Andy was a whiner. He was mean to the other children and had a paralyzingly negative attitude. No matter which activity he was assigned to, he would groan. He started every task, regardless of what it was, by sitting down and saying

"I hate this . . . do I have to do this . . . ?" I wanted to be able to meet Andy as one-caring, so I tried giving him the benefit of the doubt, cutting him slack, giving him space. Then I ran out of ideas.

His negativism was contagious: once he started complaining, the other children working near him would start doing it too. I tried to diffuse the situation with humor whenever it arose—since once Andy was laughing he forgot to be miserable. And then it dawned on me. Andy didn't really hate everything, and he didn't really mind doing the work he was assigned. Being grouchy was his "shtick"; it was the only way he knew how to enter a situation. I saw Andy in a new light, and was able to ignore his complaints and help him get settled into each new project. I don't know if my interpretation of Andy's bad attitude was correct or not, but it enabled me to find a way to interact with him that was positive and allowed me to establish a caring relationship with him. In my relationship with Andy, I moved from ethical caring to natural caring over time.

Other cases were not so easy to solve. Gus, for example, was a socially immature kindergartner with fairly advanced verbal skills. He did his very best to shirk all his academic requirements and would lie about having completed his work. He would torment any child he thought he had a chance of defeating: he would tease, insult, and bully. And, inevitably, he was the first to run to a teacher to tattle on other children.

When Martha spoke with Gus's mother about these issues at their parent-teacher conference, Frances replied, "I know. He's like that at home. The other day he wanted me to read to him and he said, 'Fran (idiot), please read to me.' He said 'idiot' under his breath, as if I couldn't hear it. When I told him that I didn't want to spend time with a boy who would call me names, he denied having done it."

It was hard to find a way to care for a child like that. I had expected to be able to enter every interaction with every student as one-caring, but I found that—in this case, at least—the realities of caring teacherly life were more complex than I had anticipated.

In the case of Andy the Whiner, I was able to draw upon ethical caring and maintain my professional commitment to the moral and intellectual relation view of teaching. However, with Gus, even ethical caring was not enough. For a number of reasons, Gus was just beyond the boundaries of my relational capabilities.

Noddings states that when an individual has the opportunity to enter into a caring relation and elects not to meet the other as one-caring, she becomes ethically diminished by that decision. In that case, I was ethically diminished by my interactions with Gus. Because I was team-teaching with Martha, however, Gus was able to find a teacher in the classroom who was able to meet him consistently as one-caring, and he did not suffer too much as a result of my inability to meet my ethical ideal.

This is an important point, and another reason why continuity, consistency, and affiliation to the program's ideals among the faculty are crucial in the Cornerstone of Caring model. If Gus were a student in my teacher education program, it would be important that he be able to be met as one-caring and affirmed in relation by other professors in the program if I were unable to do so myself.

Cornerstone 2: Intimacy-in-community

Applying the intimacy dimension of Sternberg's triangular theory of love to the process of teacher education requires some sleight of hand, given that intimacy generally occurs on a fairly small scale and teacher education does not. In the Cornerstones of Caring model of teacher education, intimacy will still represent those "close, connected, and bonded feelings" (Sternberg, 1988a, p. 120) that are found in loving relationships. However, the concept must be writ large enough to move from a one-on-one setting to the sort of large-scale intimacy that is impossible to imagine occurring anywhere but a classroom. I think of this phenomenon as intimacy-in-community.

Like intimacy as it is commonly understood, intimacy-in-community embodies trust, the sharing of meaningful experiences, a degree of mutuality and reciprocity among participants, a commitment to open communication, and depth of feeling. Unlike typical intimacy, a relation which necessitates a small number of participants, intimacy-in-community requires a large group of people sharing a common experience. In recent educational literature, intimacy-in-community is most often referred to as "creating a community of learners" or "creating a caring community in the classroom." Although the term intimacy-in-community elegantly captures the meaning I intend, in order to keep the Cornerstones of Caring model of teacher education in line with current educational parlance, I will refer to this cornerstone simply as "community."

The term community has a wide range of meanings. Even within the field of education, community can mean many different things (Merz & Furman, 1997). For our purposes, the community cornerstone will be defined in ways that align with the idea of a learning community. The characteristics of learning communities have been enumerated in many different contexts, and though the lists differ in detail, they are similar in overall effect.

The learning communities in the Fostering Communities of Learners (FCL) project developed and described by Ann Brown (1997) are characterized by agency, reflection, collaboration, and "a culture of learning, negotiating, sharing, and producing work that is displayed to others" (Brown, 1997, p. 411). The communities emerging from the National Coalition for Equality in Learning (NCEL) believe in the importance of all individuals, create collective goals that are the center of school and classroom life, share responsibility for learning and teaching, and are guided by a concern for the common good of the classroom and the school community (Trimble, 1996). Sapon-Shevin (1999) characterizes a learning community as evidencing security, open communication, mutual liking, shared goals or objectives, and connectedness and trust.

Membership in a community of learners has been determined to be an important factor in children's successful educational experiences (Brown, 1997; Trimble, 1996). By extension, it would be safe to assume that membership in a community of learners would also be an important factor in adults' successful educational experiences. The benefits of membership in a learning community—being valued, supported, challenged, encouraged, and doing the same for others, having a safe place to ask questions and to take the risk of answering questions, knowing others well and being known and respected by them in turn—are as delightful to adults as to children, and are likely to create classroom atmospheres conducive to learning and growth regardless of the age of the learners involved. Because of the close connections between the ideals of a learning community and the nature of caring encounters, the community cornerstone plays a key role in the CoC model of teacher education.

Interestingly, the role of community in preservice teacher education has been underexplored in the research literature. In their work on the impact of membership in "educative communities" on the development of reflective preservice teachers, Bullough & Gitlin (1991) discuss the importance of establishing organizational "structures which encourage more collective relations and action" (Bullough & Gitlin, 1991, p. 45). They advocate placing preservice teachers into cohort groups that remain together for the duration of their teacher education program, and then clustering cohort members at selected school sites for their field placements in order to provide cohort members with on-going opportunity for dialogue and exploration. The strategies Bullough & Gitlin outline echo Rogers & Webb's (1991) call for continuity described earlier in this chapter.

However, Oja, Diller, Corcoran & Andrew (1992) warn that "popular reference to 'cohort' groups in teacher education sometimes mean no more than sharing a common date for program matriculation" (Oja et al., 1992, p. 22). They argue instead for an approach to teacher education that hinges on the creation of "communities of support and inquiry." These communities, Oja et al. contend, must be deliberately planned and thoughtfully integrated into the philosophy of the teacher education program in order to be effective.

In discussing their novice teacher critical friendship group study, Achinstein & Meyer mention that their participants were all graduates of a teacher education program that utilized the same inquiry-oriented, community-building techniques that Achinstein & Meyer had employed in the study (Achinstein & Meyer, 1997; Meyer & Achinstein, 1998). Although Achinstein & Meyer worked with and researched their participants while the participants were enrolled in that inquiry-oriented preservice teacher education program, no published accounts exist of those preservice studies, and I was unable to find out more about the ways in which that program addressed issues of community in preservice teacher education.

It is surprising that there has been so little research focused explicitly on community in teacher education, particularly in light of the large number of textbooks available for use with preservice teachers that focus on the creation of caring learning communities with children. These texts are rooted in the belief that the preservice teachers who use the books will graduate and become teachers who will be predisposed and prepared to create caring communities with the children in their classrooms. It is easy to assume, then, that the course instructors who assign these textbooks and who have these goals for their preservice teacher education students would be likely to model these practices with the students. Perhaps they are doing so and are not researching and documenting their practices.

It is also surprising that so little attention has been paid to community in teacher education because so much attention has been paid to issues of community in teachers' working lives and in the culture of schooling. Fullan & Hargreaves decry the current state of professional community in schools, and call for teachers and principals to fight for the creation of "cultures of collaboration" (Fullan & Hargreaves, 1996, p. 48) instead. Schools characterized by a strong sense of professional community are workplaces that "create, sustain, and motivate good teachers throughout their careers" (Fullan & Hargreaves, 1996, p. 63).

Westheimer (1999) describes two specific types of teacher professional community—liberal and collective—and documents teachers' experiences working within each of these types professional communities. Sergiovanni (1994), McLaughlin (1993), Merz & Furman (1997) and many other scholars who focus on teachers' work and teacher culture (Acker, 1999; Hargreaves, 1994; Lieberman & Miller, 1984; Nias, 1989) also point to the many ways that community takes shape within and offers shape to teachers' professional lives.

It seems, then, that being part of a caring community of learners during preservice teacher education would not only offer our students the benefits of membership in a learning community and allow us to model the practices we want our students to be able to engage in with their students in the future; it would also prepare our students to participate in the kind of professional communities that will sustain them and offer them growth opportunities throughout their teaching careers. These are compelling arguments for the community cornerstone of the CoC model of teacher education.

What would community look like in a teacher education program? I suspect this might be the wrong question to ask. Community is made manifest less by the institutional arrangements of a program than by the nature of the interactions and relations among the people involved. Like many teacher educators, I have been involved in professional development school projects and other endeavors that purported to be collaborative, caring communities of one kind or another; while they may have appeared to be so on paper or on the surface, they did not feel like collaborative, caring communities to everyone involved and failed miserably as a result.

Perhaps a better question to ask would be "what would community feel like in a teacher education program?" Like caring, community is a relation. Community is enacted, community is built, and community is experienced by those involved in the process. The best that teacher educators can hope to do is to create

favorable conditions for the creation of community and then work
to nurture its growth.

Cornerstone 3: Passion

Sternberg defines passion, the third component of his triangular theory of love, as "the drives that lead to romance,
physical attraction, sexual consummation and the like" (Sternberg, 1988a, p. 120). If we use this definition, passion has little
place in a teacher education context. However, when viewed
through a different lens, passion becomes a perfectly logical
component of a teacher education program. Passion is a term
frequently associated with a teacher's love for ideas, for teaching,
and for students (hooks, 1994); passion is what separates the great
teachers from the forgettable ones (Fried, 1995). This
understanding of passion is the third cornerstone of the CoC
approach to teacher education.

One of the goals of the Cornerstones of Caring perspective on
teacher education is to communicate clearly a vision of caring as a
moral and intellectual relation that will replace the gentle smiles
and warm hugs view of caring that currently holds sway—simply
by the power of default and not because of any decisive merit—in
the field of education. Central to this endeavor is to foreground
the ways in which caring is connected to the curricular and
instructional aspects of teaching and to the intellectual energy and
expertise that teachers bring to the work they do with children.

Unfortunately, the research on caring teaching offers little to
support that goal. The empirical literature indicates that caring is
generally associated with the affective and interpersonal aspects
of classroom life and rarely connected to curriculum or
instructional practices (Hargreaves & Tucker, 1991; Weinstein,
1998).

There are a few notable exceptions. McCall (1989) offers a case
study of a student teacher who enacted child-centered pegagogies
and made specific curricular decisions that she felt would nurture
and support her students. Similarly, Rogers (1994) tells of a fourth
grade teacher who engaged students in carefully chosen, mean-

ingful learning activities because of her belief that "part of caring is providing kids with interesting and challenging things to do" (Rogers, 1994, p. 41). And, as I pointed out in chapter 1, Martha George's commitment to caring for her students shapes her curricular decision-making. As she said:

> Love guides my overall choices. I want activities that the kids will love and remember, activities that will stretch them to find out something not just about the activities but about themselves as well. More specifically, love influences my decisions because I connect what I know about each child as an individual with what activities they would particularly connect with or enjoy.

Of course, the fact that the studies describing teachers who connect caring and curriculum can be enumerated and counted on one hand illustrates just how few there are. I see this as the legacy of the gentle smiles and warm hugs view conception of caring teaching.

There is agreement that a view of caring teaching that emphasizes interpersonal relations and downplays curriculum, instruction, and classroom management is problematic and must be addressed and remedied (Hargreaves & Tucker, 1991; Weinstein, 1990, 1998). However, I must argue that point even more strongly. In order to free ourselves from the gentle smiles and warm hugs view of caring, we must make certain that our preservice teachers learn that caring teaching does not manifest itself only in interpersonal interactions.

The purpose of the passion cornerstone of the CoC model of teacher education is to replace erroneous beliefs about caring teaching with a powerful set of understandings about the fundamental connections of caring and the intellectual aspects of teachers' work. The literature on passionate teaching offers descriptions and theorizing that elegantly capture the power, the strength, and the joy that characterize the intellectual sides of caring teaching; I intend to draw on this work in developing a representation of the passion cornerstone of the CoC model.

The foremost expert on passion in teaching is Robert Fried (1995). An advocate of school reform strategies aimed at inspiring,

engaging, and motivating students, Fried points to passionate
teachers and passionate teaching as the essential elements in the
equation. He writes: "To be a passionate teacher is to be someone
in love with a field of knowledge, deeply stirred by issues and
ideas that challenge our world, drawn to the dilemmas and
potentials of the young people who come into class each day"
(Fried, 1995, p. 1). Fried asserts that "it is this quality of caring
about ideas and values, this fascination with the potential for
growth within people, this depth and fervor about doing things
well and striving for excellence" (Fried, 1995, p. 17) that sets the
passionate teachers apart from the rest of their profession.

In describing ways that teachers can be passionate, Fried
models the kind of passionate engagement he talks about:

> You can be passionate about your field of knowledge: in love with
> the poetry of Emily Dickinson or the prose of Marcus Garvey; dazzled
> by the spiral of DNA or the swirl of van Gogh's cypresses; intrigued by
> the origins of the Milky Way or the demise of the Soviet empire;
> delighted by the sound of Mozart or the sonority of French vowels; a
> maniac for health and fitness or wild about algebraic word problems . . .
> (Fried, 1995, p. 18)

Fried writes that *"passion is not just a personality trait that some
people have and others lack, but rather something discoverable, teachable,
and reproducible"* (Fried, 1995, p. 6, italics in the original). This
belief about passion makes it ideal for inclusion in the
Cornerstones of Caring model of teacher education: we can tell
students that passion is a critically important component of good
teaching and in the same breath we can assure them that passion
can—and will—be discovered and learned by each of them.

He goes on to describe two key features of the "passionate
craft of teaching" (Fried, 1995, p. 23). I include them in detail here
because this passage captures the very heart of the passion
cornerstone. Fried has linked the teacher's intellectual passion and
curricular goals with his/her desire to share meaningful,
pleasurable experiences with students and to bond with them in
creative, productive learning partnerships; this perfectly exem-

plifies practices of caring teachers working within the moral and intellectual relation view of caring:

> Passionate teachers *organize and focus* their passionate interests *by getting to the heart to their subject* and sharing with their students some of what lies there—the beauty and power that drew them to this field in the first place and that has deepened over time as they have learned and experienced more. . . . Passionate teachers *convey their passion* to novice learners—their students—*by acting as partners in learning*, rather than as experts in the field. As partners, they invite less experienced learners to search for knowledge and insightful experiences, and they build confidence and competence among students who might otherwise choose to sit back and watch their teacher do and say interesting things. (Fried, 1995, p. 23, italics in the original)

The difference between this view of caring teaching and the gentle smiles and warm hugs view is striking. This is the moral and intellectual relation view of caring that forms the foundation of the Cornerstones of Caring approach to teacher education.

From a CoC perspective, what I find most powerful about Fried's understanding of passion is its remarkable parallel to a key feature of Noddings's understanding of caring. Because of the unique ways in which these scholars have defined their terms, both passion and caring can be taught. This has tremendous implications for teacher education. Other definitions of caring and passion turn those terms into personality traits, attitudes, temperaments, dispositions that a student either has or lacks. In programs using definitions of this sort, teacher educators are left to stand by and watch the very caring and highly passionate students succeed and watch the less caring and less passionate students struggle and fail.

In a teacher education program rooted in the Cornerstones of Caring approach—and in Noddings's and Fried's definitions of caring and passion—students can learn to think of caring as a relation rather than a personality trait and can learn about the commitment that caring teachers make to meet their students as one-caring. Similarly, students can learn to connect with their intellectual passions and can learn to let those passions shine forth in their teaching. Because Noddings and Fried see caring and passion as teachable, all preservice teachers willing to learn should be able to succeed.

Jim Garrison (1997) argues that the cultivation of eros, or passionate desire, should be the supreme aim of teacher education. Although I am hesitant to offer prescriptive guidelines as to how the Cornerstones of Caring approach to teacher education should be enacted, Maxine Greene offers a view of passionate teaching so magnificent that I cannot help but include it here. Greene not only describes passionate teaching in this passage but also embodies and depicts it:

> All we can do is speak with others as passionately and eloquently as we can; all we can do is to look into each other's eyes and urge each other on to new beginnings. Our classrooms ought to be nurturing and thoughtful and just all at once; they ought to pulsate with multiple conceptions of what it is to be human and alive. They ought to resound with the voices of articulate young people in dialogues always incomplete because there is always more to be discovered and more to be said. We must want our students to achieve friendship as each one stirs to wide-awakeness, to imaginative action, and to renewed consciousness of possibility. (Greene, 1995, p. 43)

If we can create educational contexts for our preservice teachers that approximate the image Greene has presented, the passion cornerstone will be well modeled.

Implementing the Cornerstones of Caring

The commitment, community, and passion cornerstones of the CoC model are simply that: cornerstones. Any teacher education program wishing to apply the Cornerstones of Caring model in its institutional context would need to start with the cornerstones as a foundation and then build its own framework upon them.

This perspective on implementation emerges directly from Noddings's theories. Caring is a relation that is contextual, situated, and specific. The ones-caring must act toward the cared-fors in ways that are governed not by rules but by the particular needs of those receiving care. Therefore, each college and university with the desire to create a care-centered teacher education program rooted in the moral and intellectual relation view of caring, a program that capitalizes on the pedagogical power of caring and that prepares teachers to draw on that power in their work with children, must create a program that builds on these cornerstones in unique ways and meets the particular needs of the institution and its students.

But all that is the realm of theory. Now I would like to put the model to a more practical test: meeting the particular needs of the preservice teachers involved in this study. My preservice teachers faced a range of problems—the very problems that led me to feel the need to create a reconceptualized model of teacher education. My students were hindered by the limitations of their preconceptions about caring teaching; their oversimplified, essentialist, and idealistic beliefs did not serve them well in their field placements. Many of my preservice teachers were overcome by the challenges that accompany the professional instability of field experience; they suffered from exhaustion, fear, stress, and negativity, and developed closed-minded and hostile attitudes about parents and about poor families of color as a result.

Had these particular students with these specific challenges been involved in a teacher education program built upon the Cornerstones of Caring, would their experience have been significantly different? Could their problems have been prevented by commitment, community, and passion?

A fundamental feature of the Cornerstones of Caring model is the centralization of the moral and intellectual relation view of caring and the conscious and active rejection of the gentle smiles and warm hugs view of caring. This alone has the potential to have a significant impact on preservice teachers' experiences. Offering students access to the moral and intellectual relation view of caring forces them to confront and dismantle their limited preconceptions about the relationship of caring and teaching and provides them with a more useful and productive alternative. In addition, helping preservice teachers to use the moral and intellectual relation view of caring as a foundation for their professional practices will serve to shield them from the negativity and emotional drainage that accompany reliance on the gentle smiles and warm hugs view.

Each of the cornerstones in the CoC model offers preservice teachers unique benefits. Because the commitment cornerstone demands high degrees of continuity, collaboration, and affiliation to CoC ideals throughout the program, preservice teachers in a program built on the Cornerstones of Caring model are likely to receive uniform messages about caring and teaching from all faculty, cooperating teachers, and supervisors. The use of modeling, dialogue, practice, and confirmation—pedagogical strategies featured prominently in the commitment cornerstone of the CoC model—provide preservice teachers with loving, responsive teaching-learning relationships within which to consider and work through the stress, the fears, the confusion about their students' parents and any other challenges field work might pose. In addition, those loving teaching-learning relationships are also sites where preservice teachers (and teacher educators) can experience intellectual and professional growth.

The community cornerstone extends and broadens the relational benefits of the commitment cornerstone. Because of the Cornerstones of Caring model's emphasis on community, preservice teachers would have a supportive, open context in which to communicate about their challenges, struggles, questions, and successes. Sharing ideas, exchanging information, and establishing the expectation that teaching is about intellectual connection and partnership rather than isolation are other benefits of the community cornerstone.

Intellectual connection and energy are the heart of the passion cornerstone. Many of my preservice teachers—like Roberta, whose words will be reiterated here—felt burned out because they had expected teaching to involve feeling "love, love, and more love" for all the students all the time and "giving unconditional love when you are at the end of your rope." The passion cornerstone reminds preservice teachers that creativity and intellect and thinking and curriculum and instruction are central to caring teaching and relieves the strain that accompanies a view of caring that emphasizes affect alone.

I feel safe saying that this particular group of preservice teachers with their particular constellation of professional challenges would have been well served by participation in a teacher education program built on the Cornerstones of Caring model. My intent in developing the Cornerstones of Caring model was to design an approach to teacher education that would prepare teachers who will be able to draw upon a moral and intellectual relation view of caring to build a strong foundation for their professional practices and who will be able to take advantage of the pedagogical power of caring in their work with children. Embedding Noddings's notions of modeling, dialogue, practice, and confirmation within the cornerstones of commitment, community, and passion creates a theoretical model that appears capable of meeting and sustaining those goals.

Although I would love to claim that the CoC model will work for everyone in every context, I am resisting the temptation to write a victory narrative featuring swooping angels playing trumpets and singing the praises of this new approach to teacher preparation. Too many reforms have been touted as the Next Big Thing and have vanished quickly and without a trace. However, I do believe that the principles of commitment, community, and passion, when combined in creative ways by resourceful, dedicated teacher educators, will surely offer preservice teachers a stronger and more powerful foundation than we currently provide. As caring teacher educators, we must be willing to make that effort.

References

Achinstein, B. & Meyer, T. 1997. The uneasy marriage between friendship and critique: Dilemmas of fostering critical friendship in a novice teacher learning community. Paper presented at the American Educational Research Association Annual Meeting, Chicago, IL.

Acker, S. 1995. Carry on caring: The work of women teachers. *British Journal of Sociology of Education.* 16 (1): 21–36.

Acker, S. 1999. *The realities of teachers' work: Never a dull moment.* New York: Cassell & Continuum.

Alter, G. 1995. Transforming elementary social studies: The emergence of a curriculum focused on diverse, caring communities. *Theory and Research in Social Education.* 23 (4): 355–74.

Arnstine, B. 1990. Rational and caring teachers: Reconstructing teacher preparation. *Teachers College Record.* 92 (2): 230–47.

Ashton-Warner, S. 1963. *Teacher.* New York: Touchstone Books.

Ayers, W. 1993. *To teach.* New York: Teachers College Press.

Ayers, W. 1994. A teacher ain't nothin' but a hero. In P.B. Joseph & G.E. Burnaford, (Eds.), *Images of schoolteachers in twentieth-century America* (pp. 147–56). New York: St. Martin's Press.

Barbour, A. 1996. Supporting families: Children are the winners. *Early Childhood News.* 8 (6): 12–15.

Belenky, M.F., Clinchy, B.M., Goldberger, N.R. & Tarule, J.M. 1986. *Women's ways of knowing.* New York: Basic Books.

Berk, L.E. & Winsler, A. 1995. *Scaffolding children's learning: Vygotsky and early childhood education.* Washington, DC: National Association for the Education of Young Children.

Berliner, D. C. 1986. In pursuit of the expert pedagogue. *Educational Researcher.* 15(7): 5–13.

Best, S. & Kellner, D. 1991. *Postmodern theory.* New York: The Guilford Press.Biklen, S. K. 1992. Mothers gaze from teachers' eyes. In S. K. Biklen. & D. Pollard, (Eds.), *Gender and education* (pp. 155–73). Chicago: National Society for the Study of Education.

Biklen, S. K. 1995. *School work.* Albany, NY: SUNY Press.

Bodrova, E. & Leong, D.L. 1996. *Tools of the mind: The Vygotskian approach to early childhood education.* Englewood Cliffs, NJ: Prentice Hall.

Borko, H. & Mayfield, V. 1995. The roles of the cooperating teacher and university supervisor in learning to teach. *Teaching & Teacher Education.* 11 (5): 501–18.

Bozhovich, L.I. 1977. The concept of the cultural-historical development of the mind and its prospects. *Soviet Psychology.* 16 (1): 5–22.

Bredekamp, S., (Ed.). 1987. *Developmentally appropriate practice in early childhood programs serving children from birth through age 8.* Washington, D.C.: National Association for the Education of Young Children.

Bredekamp, S. and Copple, C. 1997. *Developmentally appropriate practice in early childhood programs. Revised edition.* Washington, D.C.: National Association for the Education of Young Children.

Bronfenbrenner, U. 1974. *Is early intervention effective? A report on longitudinal evaluations of preschool programs. Volume II.* Washington, D.C.: Department of Health, Education, and Welfare.

Brown, A. 1997. Transforming schools into communities of thinking and learning about serious matters. *American Psychologist.* 52 (4): 399–413.

Bullough, R.V., Jr. 1991. Exploring personal teaching metaphors in preservice teacher education. *Journal of Teacher Education.* 42 (1): 43–51.

Bullough, R.V., Jr. & Gitlin, A. 1991. Educative communities and the development of the reflective practitioner. In B.R. Tabachnick & K.M. Zeichner, (Eds.), *Issues and practices in inquiry-oriented teacher education* (pp. 35–55). London: Falmer Press.

Bullough, R.V., Jr. & Knowles, J.G. 1991. Teaching and nurturing: Changing conceptions of self as teacher in a case study of becoming a teacher. *The International Journal of Qualitative Studies in Education.* 4(2): 121–40.

Bullough, R.V., Jr. & Stokes, D.K. 1994. Analyzing personal teaching metaphors in preservice teacher education and a means for encouraging professional development. *American Educational Research Journal.* 31 (1): 197–224.

Burgess, H. & Carter, B. 1992. "Bringing out the best in people:" Teacher training and the "real" teacher. *British Journal of Sociology of Education.* 13 (3): 349–359.

Card, C. 1990. Caring and evil. *Hypatia.* 5 (1): 101–8.

Charney, R.S. 1991. *Teaching children to care.* Greenfield, MA: Northeast Foundation for Children.

Cochran-Smith, M. & Lytle, S.L. 1990. Research on teaching and teacher research: The issues that divide. *Educational Researcher.* 19 (2): 2–10.

Cole, A. L. & Knowles, J.G. 1993. Shattered images: Understanding expectations and realities of field experiences. *Teaching & Teacher Education.* 9 (5-6): 57–71.

Cole, M., John-Steiner, V., Scribner, S. & Souberman, E., (Eds.). 1978. Editors' Preface. In Vygotsky, L.S. 1978. *Mind and Society* (pp. ix-xi). Cambridge, MA: Harvard University Press.

Coleman, M. & Churchill, S. 1997. Challenges to family involvement. *Childhood Education.* 73 (3): 144–8.

Collins, P.H. 1991. *Black feminist thought.* New York: Routledge.

Connelly, F.M. & Clandinin, D.J. 1988. *Teachers as curriculum planners.* New York: Teachers College Press.

Courtney, M. 1992. Creating a caring school. *Journal of School Leadership.* 2 (1): 122–7.

Cuban, L. 1988. A fundamental puzzle of school reform. *Phi Delta Kappan.* 69 (5): 341–344.

Curcio, J.L. & First, P.F. 1995. An introduction to the journal. *Journal for a Just and Caring Education.* 1 (1): 3–4.

Daleo, M.S. 1996. *Curriculum of love.* Charlottesville, VA: Grace Publishing.

Dalton, J. & Watson, M. 1997. *Among friends: Classrooms where caring and learning prevail.* Oakland, CA: Developmental Studies Center.

Damarin, S.K. 1994. Equity, caring, and beyond: Can feminist ethics inform educational technology? *Educational Technology.* 34 (2): 34–9

Dean, A.L. 1994. Instinctual affective forces in the internalization process: Contributions of Hans Loewald. *Human Development.* 37: 42–57.

Delpit, L. 1988. The silenced dialogue: Power and pedagogy in educating other people's children. *Harvard Educational Review.* 58 (3): 280–98.

Dewey, J. 1938. *Experience and education.* New York: Collier Books.

Dewey, J. 1902/1990. *The child and the curriculum & The school and society.* Chicago:University of Chicago Press.

Diero, J.A. 1996. *Teaching with heart.* Thousand Oaks, CA: Corwin Press.

Dunkin, M.J., Precians, R.P. & Nettle, E.B. 1994. Effects of formal teacher education upon student teachers' cognitions regarding teaching. *Teaching & Teacher Education.* 10 (4): 395–408.

Dunkin, M.J. & Biddle, B.J. 1974. *The study of teaching.* New York: Holt, Rinehart & Winston.

Eaker-Rich, D. & Van Galen, J.A., (Eds.). 1996. *Caring in an unjust world: Negotiating borders and barriers in schools.* Albany, NY: SUNY Press.

Epstein, J.L. 1988. How do we improve programs for parent involvement? *Educational Horizons.* 66 (2): 58–9.

Estes, N. 1994. Learning and caring. *Executive Educator.* 16 (1): 28–30.

Forman, E. 1989. The role of peer interaction in the social construction of mathematical knowledge. *International Journal of Educational Research.* 13: 55 –69.

Foster, J.E. & Loven, R.E. 1992. The need and directions for parent involvement in the '90s: Undergraduate perspectives and expectations. *Action in Teacher Education.* 14 (3): 13–18.

Foucault, M. 1977a. Truth and power. In C. Gordon (Ed.), *Power/knowledge: Selected interviews and other writings 1972-1977. Michel Foucault* (pp. 109–133). Sussex, England: The Harvester Press.

Foucault, M. 1977b. Two lectures. In C. Gordon (Ed.), *Power/knowledge: Selected interviews and other writings 1972-1977. Michel Foucault* (pp. 78–108). Sussex, England: The Harvester Press.

Foucault, M. 1978. *The History of Sexuality, Volume 1: An Introduction.* New York: Vintage Books.

Foucault, M. 1982. The subject and power. In H. Dreyfus & P. Rabinow (Eds.), *Michel Foucault: Beyond Structuralism and Hermeneutics* (pp. 208–226). Chicago: The University of Chicago Press.

Freedman, D.M. 1999. Images of the teacher in popular culture: Pre-service teachers' critical interpretations of *Dangerous Minds. The Journal of Curriculum Theorizing.* 15 (2): 71–84.

Freedman, S. 1990. Weeding women out of "woman's true profession." In J. Antler & S.K. Biklen, (Eds.), *Changing education* (pp. 239-256). Albany, NY: SUNY Press.

Fried, R. 1995. *The passionate teacher.* Boston: Beacon Press.

Fullan, M. & Hargreaves, A. 1996. *What's worth fighting for in your school?* New York: Teachers College Press.

Garrison, J. 1997. *Dewey and Eros: Wisdom and desire in the art of teaching.* New York: Teachers College Press.

Gilligan, C. 1982. *In a different voice.* Cambridge, MA: Harvard University Press.

Goldstein, L.S. 1997. *Teaching with love: A feminist approach to early childhood education.* New York: Peter Lang Publishing.

Goldstein, L.S. 1998a. Caught in the middle: Tension and contradiction in enacting the primary grade curriculum. *Curriculum Inquiry.* 28 (3): 311–337.

Goldstein, L.S. 1998b. Teacherly love: Intimacy, commitment, and passion in classroom life. *Journal of Educational Thought.* 32 (3): 257–72.

Goldstein, L.S. 1999. The relational zone: The role of caring relationships in the co-construction of mind. *The American Educational Research Journal.* 36 (6): 647–73.

Goldstein, L.S. 2000. Luke Skywalker was my teaching assistant: Using *Star Wars* and the hero's journey metaphor in teacher education. Paper presented at the American Educational Research Association Annual Meeting, New Orleans, LA.

Gonçu, A. 1993. Development of intersubjectivity in social pretend play. Special Topic: New directions in studying pretend play." *Human Development.* 36 (4): 185–98.

Goodlad, J.I., Soder, R. & Sirotnik, K.A., (Eds.). 1990. *The moral dimensions of teaching.* San Francisco: Jossey-Bass.

Goodnow, J. 1990. The socialization of cognition: What's involved? In J.W. Stigler, R.A. Schweder, & G.H. Herdt, (Eds.), *Cultural psychology: Essays on comparative human development* (pp. 259–286). New York: Cambridge University Press.

Goodnow, J. 1993. Direction of post-Vygotskian research. In E.A. Forman, N. Minick & C.A. Stone, (Eds.), *Contexts for learning: Sociocultural dynamics in children's development* (pp. 369–381). New York: Oxford University Press.

Gootman, M.E. 1997. *The caring teacher's guide to discipline.* Thousand Oaks, CA: Corwin Press.

Gore, J. 1993. *The struggle for pedagogies: Critical and feminist discourses as regimes of truth.* New York: Routledge.

Graham, P. 1999. Powerful influences: A case of one student teacher renegotiating his perceptions of power relations. *Teaching & Teacher Education.* 15 (5)" 523–40.

Greenwood, G.E. & Hickman, C.W. 1991. Research and practice in parent involvement: Implications for teacher education. *The Elementary School Journal.* 91 (3): 279–88.

Greene, M. 1973. *Teacher as stranger.* Belmont, CA: Wadsworth Publishing Company.

Greene, M. 1978. *Landscapes of learning.* New York: Teachers College Press.

Greene, M. 1995. *Releasing the imagination: Essays on education, the arts, and social change.* San Francisco: Jossey-Bass.

Grossman, P.L. & Richert, A.E. 1988. Unacknowledged knowledge growth: A re-examination of the effects of teacher education. *Teaching & Teacher Education.* 4 (1): 53–62.

Grumet, M. 1988. *Bitter milk.* Amherst, MA: University of Massachusetts Press.

Hargreaves, A. 1994. *Changing teachers, changing times.* London: Cassell.

Hargreaves, A. & Tucker, E. 1991. Teaching and guilt: Exploring the feelings of teaching. *Teaching & Teacher Education.* 7 (5/6): 491–505.

Held, V. 1987. Feminism and moral theory. In E.F. Kittay & D.T. Meyers, (Eds.), *Women and moral theory* (pp. 111–128). Totowa, NJ: Rowman and Littlefield.

Henderson, J. G. 1988. An ethic of caring applied to reflective professional development. *Teaching Education.* 2(1): 91–5.

Hoagland, S.L. 1990. Some concerns about Nel Noddings' *Caring. Hypatia.* 5 (1): 109–14.

Hollingsworth, S. 1989. Prior beliefs and cognitive change in learning to teach. *American Educational Research Journal.* 26 (2): 160–89.

hooks, b. 1994. *Teaching to transgress: Education as the practice of freedom.* New York: Routledge.

Hoover-Dempsey, K.V., Bassler, O.C. & Brissie, J.S. 1987. Parent involvement: Contributions of teacher efficacy, school socioeconomic status, and other school characteristics. *American Educational Research Journal.* 24 (3): 417–35.

Hoy, W.K. & Rees, R. 1977. The bureaucratic socialization of student teachers. *Journal of Teacher Education.* 28 (1): 23–6.

Hoy, W.K. & Woolfolk, A.E. 1990. Socialization of student teachers. *American Educational Research Journal.* 27 (2): 279–300.

Isenberg, J. 1994. *Going by the book: The role of popular classroom chronicles in the professional development of teachers.* Westport, CT: Bergin & Garvey.

Jelinek, C.A. 1986. Stress and the preservice teacher. *Teacher Educator.* 22 (1): 2–8.

Joseph, P.B., & Burnaford, G.E., (Eds.). 1994. *Images of schoolteachers in twentieth-century America.* New York: St. Martin's Press.

Kagan, D.M. 1992. Professional growth among preservice and beginning teachers. *Review of Educational Research.* 62: 129–69.

Kahne, J. & Westheimer, J. 1992. Building community: A model for teacher education and staff development. Paper presented at the American Educational Research Association Annual Meeting, San Francisco, CA.

Katz, L.G. 1971. Sentimentality in preschool teachers: Some possible interpretations. *Peabody Journal of Education.* 48 (2): 96–105.

Kaufman, B. 1964. *Up the down staircase.* New York: Avon Books.

Kaye, K. 1982. *The mental and social life of babies.* Chicago: University of Chicago Press.

Knowles, J.G. & Holt-Reynolds, D. 1991. Shaping pedagogies against personal histories in preservice teacher education. *Teachers College Record.* 93: 87–113.

Kohl, H. 1984. *Growing minds.* New York: Harper & Row.

Lamme, L.L., & McKinley, L. 1992. Creating a caring classroom with children's literature. *Young Children.* 48 (1): 65–71.

Larrabee, M.J., (Ed.). 1993. *An ethic of care.* New York: Routledge.

Lave, J. & Wenger, E. 1991. *Situated learning: Legitimate peripheral participation.* Cambridge: Cambridge University Press.

Leavitt, R.L. 1994. *Power and emotion in infant-toddler day care.* Albany, NY: SUNY Press.

Levin, M. 1987. Parent-teacher collaboration. In D.W. Livingstone, (Ed.), *Critical pedagogy and cultural power* (pp. 269–291). South Hadley, MA: Bergen and Garvey.

Lieberman, A. & Miller, L. 1984. *Teachers, their world, and their work: Implications for school improvement.* Alexandria, VA: Association for Supervision and Curriculum Development.

Lightfoot, S.L. 1977. Family-school interactions: The cultural image of mothers and teachers. *Signs: Journal of Women in Culture and Society.* 3 (2): 395–408.

Lipsitz, J. 1995. Prologue: Why we should care about caring. *Phi Delta Kappan.* 76 (9): 665–66.

Litowitz, B.E. 1993. Deconstruction in the zone of proximal development. In E.A. Forman, N. Minick & C.A. Stone, (Eds.), *Contexts for learning: Sociocultural dynamics in children's development* (pp. 184–196). New York: Oxford University Press.

Lortie, D.C. 1975. *Schoolteacher: A sociological study.* Chicago: University of Chicago Press.

Lucas, G. (Screenwriter & Director). 1999. *Star Wars Episode I: The Phantom Menace.* [Film.] Los Angeles: 20th Century Fox.

Maas. J. 1991. Writing and reflection in teacher education. In B.R. Tabachnick & K.M. Zeichner (eds.), *Issues and practices in inquiry-oriented teacher education* (pp. 211-225). London: Falmer.

MacDonald, C.J. 1993. Coping with stress during the teaching practicum: The student teacher's perspective. *Alberta Journal of Educational Research.* 39 (4): 407–18.

Martin, L.M.W. 1990. Detecting and defining science problems: A study of video-mediated lessons. In L.C. Moll, (Ed.), *Vygotsky and education: Instructional implications and applications of sociohistorical psychology* (pp. 374–402). New York: Cambridge University Press.

McCall, A.L. 1989. Care and nurturance in teaching: A case study. *Journal of Teacher Education.* 40 (1): 39–44.

McDermott, R.P. 1977. Social relations as contexts for learning in school. *Harvard Educational Review.* 47 (2): 198–213.

McIntyre, A. 1997. Constructing an image of a white teacher. *Teachers College Record.* 98 (4): 653–81.

McIntyre, S.R. & Tlusty, R.H. 1995. Computer-mediated discourse: Electronic dialogue journaling and reflective practice. Paper presented at the American Educational Research Association annual meeting, San Francisco, CA.

McLaren, P. 1994. *Life in schools*. New York: Longman. McLaughlin, H.J. 1991. Reconciling care and control: Authority in classroom relationships. *Journal of Teacher Education.* 42 (3): 182–95.

McLaughlin, H.J. 1991. Reconciling care and control: Authority in classroom relationships. *Journal of Teacher Education.* 42(3): 182-95.

McLaughlin, M. 1993. What matters most in teachers' workplace context? In J.W. Little and M. McLaughlin (Eds.), *Teachers' work* (pp. 79-103). New York: Teachers College Press.

McPherson, G.H. 1972. *Small town teacher.* Cambridge, MA: Harvard University Press.

Memmi, A. 1965. *The colonizer and the colonized.* Boston: Beacon Press.

Merz, C. & Furman, G. 1997. *Community and schools: Promise and paradox.* New York: Teachers College Press.

Meyer, T. & Achinstein, B. 1998. Collaborative inquiry among novice teachers as professional development: Sustaining habits of heart and mind. Paper presented at the American Educational Research Association Annual Meeting, San Diego, CA.

Moles, O.C. 1982. Synthesis of recent research on parent participation in children's education. *Educational Leadership.* 40 (2): 44–47.

Moll, L.C. 1990. Introduction. In L.C. Moll, (Ed.), *Vygotsky and education: Instructional implications and applications of sociohistorical psychology* (pp. 1-27). New York: Cambridge University Press.

Moll, L.C. & Greenberg, J.B. 1990. Creating zones of possibilities: Combining social contexts for instruction. In L.C. Moll, (Ed.), *Vygotsky and education: Instructional implications and applications of sociohistorical psychology* (pp. 319-348). New York: Cambridge University Press.

Moll, L.C. & Whitmore, K.F. 1993. Vygotsky in classroom practice: Moving from individual transmission to social transaction. In E.A. Forman, N. Minick & C.A. Stone, (Eds.), *Contexts for learning: Sociocultural dynamics in children's development* (pp. 19-42). New York: Oxford University Press.

Nelson, M.K. 1994. Family day care providers: Dilemmas of daily practice. In E.N. Glenn, G. Chang, & L.R. Forcey, (Eds.), *Mothering: Ideology, experience, and agency* (pp. 181-209). New York: Routledge.

Nettle, E.B. 1998. Stability and change in the beliefs of student teachers during practice teaching. *Teaching & Teacher Education.* 14 (2): 193-204.

Newman, D., Griffin, P. & Cole, M. 1989. *The construction zone: Working for cognitive change in school.* Cambridge: Cambridge University Press.

Newman, F. & Holzman, L. 1993. *Lev Vygotsky: Revolutionary scientist.* New York: Routledge.

Newson, J. & Newson, E. 1975. Intersubjectivity and the transmission of culture: On the social origins of symbolic functioning. *Bulletin of the British Psychological Society.* 28: 437–446.

Nias, J. 1989. *Primary teachers talking.* London: Routledge.

Noblit, G.W. 1993. Power and caring. *American Educational Research Journal.* (30): 1. 23–38.

Noddings, N. 1984. *Caring: A feminine approach to ethics and education.* Berkeley: University of California Press.

Noddings, N. 1986. Fidelity in teaching, teacher education, and research for teaching. *Harvard Educational Review.* 56 (4): 496–510.

Noddings, N. 1992. *The challenge to care in schools.* New York: Teachers College Press.

Noddings, N. 1999. Caring and competence. In G. Griffin, (Ed.), *The education of teachers: Ninety-eighth yearbook for the National Society for the Study of Education* (pp. 205–220). Chicago: University of Chicago Press.

Oja, S., Diller, A., Corcoran, E. & Andrew, M.D. 1992. Communities of inquiry, communities of support: The five year teacher education program at the University of New Hampshire. In L. Valli, (Ed.), *Reflective Teacher Education: Cases and critiques* (pp. 3–23). Albany, NY: SUNY Press.

Packer, M.J. 1993. Commentary: Away from internalization. In E.A. Forman, N. Minick & C.A. Stone, (Eds.), *Contexts for learning: Sociocultural dynamics in children's development* (pp. 254–265). New York: Oxford University Press.

Palincsar, A.M., Brown, A.L. & Campione, J.C. 1993. First-grade dialogues for knowledge acquisition and use. In E.A. Forman, N. Minick & C.A. Stone, (Eds.), *Contexts for learning: Sociocultural dynamics in children's development* (pp. 43–58). New York: Oxford University Press.

Peterson, R. 1992. *Life in a crowded place.* Portsmouth, NH: Heinemann.

Powell, D.R. & Diamond, K.E. 1995. Approaches to parent-teacher relationships in US. early childhood programs during the twentieth century. *Journal of Education.* 177 (3): 71–94.

Prillaman, A.R., Eaker, D.J., and Kendrick, D.M., (Eds.). 1994. *The tapestry of caring.* Norwood, NJ: Ablex Publishing.

Rasinski, T.V. 1990. Aspects of a caring reading curriculum. *Reading Horizons.* 31 (2): 127–37.

Ribbens, J. 1993. Standing by the school gate—the boundaries of maternal authority? In M. David, R. Edwards, M. Hughes & J. Ribbens, (Eds.), *Mothers and education: Inside out?* (pp. 59–90). New York: St. Martin's Press.

Robicheaux, R. 1996. Professional development: Caring teachers can realize the vision of the standards. *Mathematics Teaching in the Middle School.* 1(9): 738–42.

Rogers, D.L. 1994. Conceptions of caring in a fourth grade classroom. In A.R. Prillaman, D.J. Eaker, & D.M. Kendrick, (Eds.), *The tapestry of caring* (pp. 33–47). Norwood, NJ: Ablex Publishing.

Rogers, D., & Webb, J. 1991. The ethic of caring in teacher education. *Journal of Teacher Education.* 42 (3): 173–81.

Rogoff, B. 1986. Adult assistance of children's learning. In T.E. Raphael, (Ed.), *The contexts of school-based literacy* (pp. 27–40). New York: Random House.

Rogoff, B. 1990. *Apprenticeship in thinking: Cognitive development in social context.* New York: Oxford University Press.

Rogoff, B., Malkin, C., & Gilbride, K. 1984. Interaction with babies as guidance in development. In B. Rogoff & J.V. Wertsch, (Eds.), *Children's learning in the "zone of proximal development"* (pp. 31–44). San Francisco: Jossey-Bass.

Rogoff, B. & Wertsch, J.V. 1984. Editors' notes. In B. Rogoff & J.V. Wertsch, (Eds.), *Children's learning in the "zone of proximal development"* (pp. 1–6). San Francisco: Jossey-Bass.

Rommetveit, R. 1974. *On message structure: a framework for the study of language and communication.* New York: Wiley.

Rosiek, J. 1994. Caring, classroom management, and teacher education: The need for case study and narrative methods. *Teaching Education.* 6 (1): 21–30.

Ruddick, S. 1989. *Maternal thinking.* Boston: Beacon Press.

Rust, F.O. 1994. Toward a curriculum of caring and cooperation for elementary social education. *Social Science Record.* 31 (1): 7–9.

Sapon-Shevin, M. 1999. *Because we can change the world.* Boston, MA: Allyn & Bacon.

Sergiovanni, T.J. 1994. *Building community in schools.* San Francisco: Jossey-Bass.

Shulman, L.S. 1986. Those who understand: Knowledge growth in teaching. *Educational Researcher.* 15 (2): 4–14.

Sickle, M.V., & Spector, B. 1996. Caring relationships in science classrooms: A symbolic interaction study. *Journal of Research in Science Teaching.* 33 (4): 433–53.

Silvernail, D.L. & Costello, M.H. 1983. The impact of student teaching and internship programs on preservice teachers' pupil control perspectives, anxiety levels, and teaching concerns. *Journal of Teacher Education.* 34 (4): 32–36.

Sternberg, R. J. 1988a. *The triangle of love.* New York: Basic Books.

Sternberg, R.J. 1988b. Triangulating love. In R.J. Sternberg & M.L. Barnes, (Eds.), *The psychology of love* (pp. 119–138). New Haven: Yale University Press.

Stone, C. A. 1993. What is missing in the metaphor of scaffolding? In E.A. Forman, N. Minick & C.A. Stone, (Eds.), *Contexts for learning: Sociocultural dynamics in children's development* (pp. 169–183). New York: Oxford University Press.

Swadener, E.B. 1992. Comment made during discussion at conference Reconceptualizing Early Childhood Education: Theory, Research, and Practice. Chicago, IL.

Swick, K.J. 1999. Service learning helps future teachers strengthen caring perspectives. *The Clearing House.* 73 (1): 29–32.

Tabachnick, B.R. & Zeichner, K.M. 1984. The impact of the student teaching experience on the development of teacher perspectives. *Journal of Teacher Education.* 35 (6): 28–36.

Tella, S. 1992. Talking shop via email: A thematic linguistic analysis of electronic mail communication. University of Helsinki, Department of Teacher Education, Helsinki, Finland. (ERIC Document Reproduction Service No. ED 352 015).

Tharp, R. 1993. Institutional and social context of educational practice and reform. In E.A. Forman, N. Minick & C.A. Stone, (Eds.), *Contexts for learning: Sociocultural dynamics in children's development* (pp. 269–282). New York: Oxford University Press.

Thayer-Bacon, B.J., Arnold, S. & Stoots, J. 1998. Identification of caring professors in teacher education programs. ERIC Document No. 418 970.

Thayer-Bacon, B.J. & Bacon, C.S. 1996. Caring professors: A model. *The Journal of General Education.* 45 (4): 255–269. Thayer-Bacon, B.J. 1996b. Caring in the college/university classroom. *Educational Foundations.* 10 (2): 53–72.

Thurer, S.L. 1991. *The myths of motherhood.* Boston: Houghton Mifflin.

Trimble, K. 1996. Building a learning community. *Equity & Excellence in Education.* 29 (1): 37–40.

Tronto, J.C. 1993. *Moral boundaries: A political argument for an ethic of care.* New York: Routledge.

van der Veer, R. & Valsiner, J., (Eds.). 1994. *The Vygotsky reader.* Cambridge, MA: Blackwell.

Vygotsky, L.S. 1962. *Thought and language.* Cambridge, MA: The M.I.T. Press.

Vygotsky, L.S. 1978. *Mind and society.* Cambridge, MA: Harvard University Press.

Vygotsky, L.S. & Luria, A. 1994. Tool and symbol in child development. In R. van der Veer & J. Valsiner, (Eds.), *The Vygotsky reader* (pp. 99–174). Cambridge, MA: Blackwell.

Walkerdine, V. 1986. Progressive pedagogy and political struggle. *Screen.* 27: 54–60.

Weber S., & Mitchell, C. (1995). *That's funny, you don't look like a teacher.* Washington, DC: The Falmer Press.

Weinstein, C.S. 1990. Prospective elementary teachers' beliefs about teaching: Implications for teacher education. *Teaching & Teacher Education.* 6 (3): 279–90.

Weinstein, C.S. 1998. "I want to be nice, but I have to be mean": Exploring prospective teachers' conceptions of caring and order. *Teaching & Teacher Education.* 14 (2): 153–63.

Wertsch, J.V. 1979. From social interaction to higher psychological processes: A clarification and application of Vygotsky's theory. *Human Development.* 22: 1–22.

Wertsch, J.V. 1984. The zone of proximal development: Some conceptual issues. In B. Rogoff & J.V. Wertsch, (Eds.), *Children's learning in the "zone of proximal development"* (pp. 7–18). San Francisco: Jossey-Bass.

Wertsch, J.V. 1985. *Vygotsky and the social formation of the mind.* Cambridge, MA: Harvard University Press.

Wertsch, J.V. 1991. A sociocultural approach to socially shared cognition. In L.B. Resnick, J.M. Levine & S.D. Teasley (Eds.), *Perspectives on Socially Shared Cognition,* (pp. 85–100). Washington D.C.: American Psychological Association.

Westheimer, J. 1999. Communities and consequences: An inquiry into ideology and practice in teachers' professional work. *Educational Administration*

Quarterly. 35 (1): 71–105.

Wilson, S.M. & Wineburg, S.S. 1993. Wrinkles in time and place: Using performance assessments to understand the knowledge of history teachers. *American Educational Research Journal*. 30 (4): 729–69.

Wood, D., Bruner, J.S., & Ross, G. 1976. The role of tutoring in problem solving. *Journal of Child Psychology and Psychiatry*. 17: 89–100.

Wood, D. & Middleton, D. 1975. A study of assisted problem-solving. *British Journal of Psychology*. 66 (2): 181–191.

Zeichner, K.M. 1980. Myths and realities: Field-based experiences in preservice teacher education. *Journal of Teacher Education*. 31 (6): 45–9, 51–55.

Zeichner, K.M. & Grant, C.A. 1991. Biography and social structure in the socialization of student teachers: a re-examination of the pupil control ideologies of student teachers. *Journal of Education for Teaching*. 7 (3): 298–314.

Zeichner, K.M. & Tabachnick, B.R. 1981. Are the effects of university teacher education "washed out" by school experience? *Journal of Teacher Education*. 32 (3): 7–11.

Index

RETHINKING CHILDHOOD

JOE L. KINCHELOE & JANICE A. JIPSON, *General Editors*

A revolution is occurring regarding the study of childhood. Traditional notions of child development are under attack, as are the methods by which children are studied. At the same time, the nature of childhood itself is changing as children gain access to information once reserved for adults only. Technological innovations, media, and electronic information have narrowed the distinction between adults and children, forcing educators to rethink the world of schooling in this new context.

This series of textbooks and monographs encourages scholarship in all of these areas, eliciting critical investigations in developmental psychology, early childhood education, multicultural education, and cultural studies of childhood.

Proposals and manuscripts may be sent to the general editors:

> Joe L. Kincheloe
> c/o Peter Lang Publishing, Inc.
> 275 Seventh Avenue, 28th floor
> New York, New York 10001
>
> *or*
>
> Janice A. Jipson
> 219 Pease Court
> Janesville, WI 53545

To order other books in this series, please contact our Customer Service Department at:

> (800) 770-LANG (within the U.S.)
> (212) 647-7706 (outside the U.S.)
> (212) 647-7707 FAX

Or browse online by series at:
> www.peterlangusa.com